# GOWER ROCK

## STUART LLEWELLYN & MATT WOODFIELD

First published in Great Britain 2012 by Pesda Press

Tan y Coed Canol

Ceunant

Caernarfon

Gwynedd

LL55 4RN

Maps – Bute Cartographic

Contains Ordnance Survey data © Crown copyright and database right 2012

ISBN:   978-1-906095-36-9

Printed and bound in Poland. www.hussarbooks.pl

# GOWER ROCK

*Gower Rock* aims to showcase the depth and quality of rock climbing on this wild, beautiful yet somewhat unknown peninsula. The book's development has been inspired both by local enthusiasm and the absence of a modern guidebook to the area. While we love the tranquillity of the crags and the absence of queues, we also want to share this really rather special place with others. The area has been crying out for a modern guidebook for many years, and now you hold it in your hands. We hope it will lead you into new and exciting places where adventure, challenge and excitement are all part of the experience.

It is perhaps because of the absence of just such a guide that Gower is often overlooked. This is a genuine shame as the area contains a wide variety of climbing on an enticing array of venues. On some routes you can step straight off golden sands onto classic lines; in other cases you can wend your way across peaceful cliff-top paths before dropping into some pretty demanding terrain just a stone's throw from ice-cream-scoffing tourists and pastoral picnic spots.

To most climbers, coastal climbing in South Wales means Pembrokeshire. After glancing through these full-colour topos and drooling over the inspirational photographs, we hope that you'll reconsider driving past that wiggly bit of coast just before the M4 ends and spend some of your time on our cliffs and crags.

The magnificent areas of Fall Bay and Three Cliffs have enough classic routes to keep you busy on many visits to the peninsula. The sport crags of Southgate compliment and add variety to the well-established hard routes of Oxwich and Pwlldu. The selection of venues and climbs included in this guide will provide plenty of adventure for all climbers, among some of the best scenery in the UK. In a letter to his girlfriend, Swansea's poet son Dylan Thomas described Gower as: "GOWER is a very beautiful peninsula, some miles from this blowsy town… as a matter of fact it is one of the loveliest sea-coast stretches in the whole of Britain".

In 1956 the Gower peninsula was designated as the UK's first Area of Outstanding Natural Beauty (AONB).

Any visitor to the area will see why: it is packed full of stunning beaches and welcoming villages, and provides a breath-taking backdrop to numerous outdoor activities including surfing and paragliding. There are miles of fantastic coastal paths to walk along (a perfect way to explore the many treats of the peninsula) and copious amounts of climbing.

The spark that ignited this guidebook was the creation of a dozen topos for the British Mountaineering Council (BMC) Gower Climbing Festival, which debuted in 2009. The aim of this event is to promote climbing on the peninsula, drawing climbers from all over the UK for one weekend in September to celebrate Gower climbing while raising money for the Royal National Lifeboat Institution (RNLI), the Coastguard and the South Wales Bolt Fund (SWBF).

☐ The first BMC Gower Climbing Festival.

# ACKNOWLEDGEMENTS

Many individuals have contributed to the finished book you hold in your hands. A core collection of climbers have helped the two authors massively by providing feedback on the routes, topos and approaches and contributing to the contents of the book: to John Bullock, Stefan Doerr, Nik Goile, Martin Kocsis, Simon Rawlinson, Simon Robinson and Steve 'Sparky' Warrington, thank you!

A handful of photographers deserve special praise for the exciting look of this guide, and we are very grateful to be allowed to use images from your collections. Gower now has a deserving modern guidebook full of inspirational imagery, a match for any other area in the UK. Our thanks must go to: Simon Rawlinson (www.makethenextmove.co.uk), Chris Allen (www.rockall.biz), Carl Ryan (Red Mist Extreme photography) and Wayne Tucker. Thank you to all who posed for the photos; we hope you like the shots as much as we do.

We must also thank those that kindly sat and read through the endless scripts which were the bare bones of the book, before the creation of this colourful and glossy sleek-finished guide: Becky Bailey, Donna Carless, Gwyn Evans and Ben Tiffin.

Personal thanks from Stuart must go to Christopher Mathewson, who helped in the early stages of approaching a publisher and the hours you spent guiding Stuart and the project.

We would also like to extend special thanks to Elfyn Jones (BMC) and Sian Musgrave (National Trust) for assistance and guidance with the Access and Conservation notes, and Charles Romijn for his brilliantly drawn and entertaining cartoons. Our kind thanks also go to the following people for their various contributions and support: Berwyn Evans, David Garnett, Tom Hill, Tom Hutton, Tony Rees, Andy Sharp, Dave Sperring and Roy Thomas.

A final word of thanks must go to our publisher Franco Ferrero for giving us this opportunity. You no longer have an excuse not to have experienced Gower Rock!

The Worm at sunset.
Photo: Stuart Llewellyn.

The Worm.
Photo: Wayne Tucker.

# CONTENTS

# USING THE GUIDE

This aim of this book is to be a modern selective guide, showcasing the best climbing Gower has to offer. We have attempted to profile the best on show for trad, sport, bouldering and even some deepwater solos. Where a crag has been included, the majority of routes have been described (unless they are of poor quality). In the case of sport crags, all lines have been included to avoid confusion. This approach, akin to the recent trend of other guidebooks, is designed to make this a useful and practical guide to help people get out and climb.

All route information is presented in the following style:

 **Example Route**　　　　　　　**20m VS 4c**

*FA A. Climber & A.N. Other 1982*

The first line is route name, difficulty and length, with the number relating to the photo topo. Details of the first ascent team, and date climbed, are provided in the second line. Additional information to compliment the photo topo is then provided in the description; don't forget to read any notes about tides, access or descents.

## GETTING THERE

The approach to each venue is described at the start of the chapter, and assumes use of the peninsula map on the inside cover of the book to help get you close.

Where the parking is not so obvious, each chapter has further details to help you find the intended spot. There is an accompanying approach map to get you from your car to the crag. Several of the areas can be reached by bus from the main bus station in Swansea.

## OTHER GUIDEBOOKS

The guidebook team would like to acknowledge the efforts of all the climbers who have worked on documenting the climbing on the Gower peninsula over the years, from the very first guide book (Jeremy Talbot's 1970 *Gower Peninsula*) to the many comprehensive guides since produced by the South Wales Mountaineering Club (SWMC) including the 2003 edition by Roy Thomas and Goi Ashmore. Adrian Berry's *Rockfax miniGuide* is a recent update for the area, documenting sport climbing developments. Without these books and the information they contain, we wouldn't have climbed in this wonderful area and been able to document the routes for this guidebook. In recent years the SWMC has made a lot of this information freely available on their website, with climbers submitting up-to-date new route information for not only the Gower but the vast Southeast Wales area. Search online for 'SWMC wiki'.

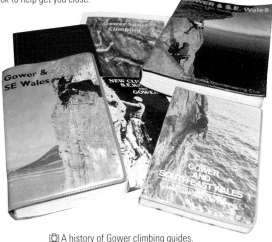

📷 A history of Gower climbing guides.

## BOULDERING

Dotted between the detailed pages of the main climbing areas, suggestions of bouldering venues along the peninsula are also included for you to seek out and crank! Descriptions of where to park, tidal status and approaches are included, but in general we recommend simply exploring (that's half the fun). For those who do want an itinerary of problems search online for 'SWMC wiki', where a great collection of information can be found.

**Bouldering mats:** Highly recommended; it must also be emphasised that in some venues the top outs are loose.

## GRADES AND LINES

In compiling this book the team has consulted with numerous local climbers and also checked with the voting system on UKClimbing.com in an attempt to obtain a consensus on grades. Personal climbing experience and numerous crag visits were used to check the lines drawn on the topos, but it is inevitable that there are some errors; you should always use your own judgement.

Photo: Rockall Images.

## HELMETS

It's highly recommended to wear helmets when climbing as a large proportion of Gower crags have loose sections of rock (even the premium venues featured here).

## ETHICS, STYLES AND DEVELOPMENTS

The whole array of climbing styles can be found on the peninsula, from pure traditional climbs (some with in situ pegs) to fully equipped sport routes. The area is covered by a detailed bolt policy on a crag-by-crag basis, which can be found on the South Wales Bolt Fund (SWBF) website (www.southwalesboltfund.co.uk). For those wanting to develop bolted routes, a process is in place facilitated by local BMC volunteers to allow consultation with the local climbing community and the appropriate landowner. To contact the local access representative, visit the BMC website (www.thebmc.co.uk) and search for 'Access & Conservation'. Alternatively, contact the BMC office.

## PEGS, BOLTS AND OTHER FIXED GEAR

As with other sea cliff venues, the conditions of pegs and in situ threads must be treated with major caution. It's entirely possible that these are the original bits of gear from the first ascent, which have been subjected to years of weathering and corrosion in a marine environment. You may also come across remnants of someone's trad rack which the second has not been able to retrieve; the same caution must be applied.

A mixture of bolts will be found on the sport routes of Gower, from expansion bolts with hangers to various different glue-in designs.

[📷] The 'twizzle' glue-in and expansion bolt and hanger combo.

The majority of these bolts were funded by the first ascensionists when they developed the climb. Since the re-awakening of the SWBF, some of the long-established sport-climbing venues have had their ageing bolts replaced. At the time of writing, Foxhole and parts of Oxwich have been reequipped by willing volunteers with kit provided by the fund.

To make a donation to bolt funds, visit the SWBF website. Alternatively, there are donation boxes at Dynamic Rock (Swansea) and Boulders (Cardiff) climbing centres. Thanks in advance for any donations you may give.

[📷] Hopefully a rare sight on Gower sport climbs.

## GOWER NUGGETS

Dotted in and around the book are some nuggets of knowledge from the team about Gower's geological, human and climbing history. It is hoped that you find these interesting, or at least useful for dropping into the conversion in the pub after your day's climbing.

## CONTACT THE AUTHORS

A lot of effort has gone into ensuring that the information in this guide is relevant, accurate and informative. If you spot any errors or inaccuracies (or simply had a good day out!) please feel free to send your feedback to gower.rock@gmail.com.

# ACCESS & CONSERVATION

## WHAT MAKES GOWER SPECIAL?

The Gower Peninsular is home to a wide variety of natural history dating back some 400 million years and a human history dating back 33,000 years (see Paviland Valley). Nesting peregrines (the fastest creatures on the planet) and rare plants that grow nowhere else in the UK can be found, and a record of the developing planet is held within the rock beds and cave sediments around the coast. The species and landforms found on the Gower cliffs provide a stunning and impressive backdrop to the climbing sites, and it's in everyone's interests to do what we can to protect these incredible sites for future generations.

## WHAT PROTECTS GOWER?

Almost the whole of the South Gower coast is designated as a Site of Special Scientific Interest (SSSI), in order to provide legal protection for its conservation. An area can become a SSSI for its rare fauna and flora such as rare plants or nesting birds or its geophysical features.

All land is owned by somebody and the inclusion of a venue in this guide does not imply that you have the right to go there. There are no known access issues at any of the venues in this guide, but climbers have an obvious vested interest in acting responsibly. This includes responsible parking, taking litter home, respecting SSSIs, following nesting restrictions and generally keeping a low profile.

## KEEPING OUT OF TROUBLE

Given the SSSI status, it could be deemed illegal to recklessly damage or disturb the key conservation features of the site.

It is a criminal offence to disturb any nesting bird or to damage any nest site while it is in use. The bird restrictions noted in this guide protect the nesting sites for important species to prevent their further decline. Always be aware of the impact your action may be having on the wildlife and landscape around you. Activities such as route cleaning, modifying the rock face and placing bolts could cause damage to the protected features, and permission from the landowner should be sought. For more information on new routes please see the section on 'Ethics, styles and developments' above.

If you do encounter any problems with access while out on the cliffs of Gower, then please do not antagonise the landowner or other organisations. The best course of action is to refer the issue to the BMC via their regional access database (RAD; www.thebmc.co.uk/bmccrag), where excellent up-to-date information can be found.

## FEATHERED FRIENDS

The cliffs of Gower are renowned for their bird populations. Some are present year round, while others are spring and summer visitors only. If you hear obviously distressed birds screeching or flying around in an agitated manner, especially during the nesting season, it's highly likely that you are causing a disturbance. If this is the case, then move away from the site as quickly and safely as possible. It takes as little as 20 minutes for abandoned eggs to chill and for the chicks to die.

> Nesting Restrictions are in place 1st March–15th August at Yellow Wall and Thurba Head. These restrictions are sometimes lifted earlier once nesting finishes; see the BMC RAD for up-to-date information.

There are many different species present on the cliffs, each with their own special requirements. The following are just a small selection of the birds found on Gower.

### Chough

📷 Chough (ch-uff). Photo: Barry Stewart.

The chough (a small crow) is easily identified by its red beak and feet. This nationally rare bird is a sociable and year-round resident. They only nest at a handful of sites on the peninsula, normally around March and occasionally a second attempt as late as June.

### Peregrine falcon

The peregrine falcon feeds on small mammals and other birds. It has a distinct high-pitched shriek and hunts by hovering effortlessly until its prey is spotted. They nest on rocky ledges and cover the surrounding rock in white guano. They are the fastest creature on the planet, reaching speeds of over 200mph during their hunting swoop. The sound when they hit their prey is unforgettable.

### Razorbill

📷 Razorbill. Photo: Barry Stewart.

Razorbills are members of the auk family, seabirds which only come to land for nesting. A large colony resides on Worms Head, alongside the guillemots and seals.

### Others

Other species found on Gower include kittiwakes (which are becoming more endangered and nationally scarcer), various gulls and cormorants. The ubiquitous fulmar is always present on the Gower cliffs, and is a bird that climbers do not need to be reminded to avoid. It has a very accurately delivered defence mechanism of puking a putrid and stinking goo over any climber that inadvertently gets too close!

# SAFETY & ACCIDENTS

## GETTING HELP

Mobile signal is variable, but often better on the cliff tops than at the base. Dial 999 and ask for the Coastguard; these are the best people for the job of organising a rescue and know the area well.

Give as much information as you can, including location (area, bay, cliff, nearest road, etc.) and casualty condition. Keep the casualty alive and warm until help arrives. This is much easier if you know what you're doing; attending an Emergency First Aid course can save lives!

## TIDES

Many of the crags in this guide are affected by the sea, some more than others, but all need the same respect, knowledge and planning. The information given on access to tidal crags is a rough guide based on an average tide, but this does not take into account any other influences. The impact of the sea on these crags is a result of the combined effects of the tide and weather.

The gravitational pull of the moon and sun create a 'bulge' in the sea on opposite sides of the planet. If the sun and moon work together and pull in the same (or directly opposite) direction we experience larger 'spring' tides; if they pull in different directions then we see smaller 'neap' tides. Due to the regularity of the moon's orbit around our planet and our planet's around the sun, the time and height of the tide can be predicted. There are two high tides and two low tides every day, occurring around 6 hours apart. The geography of the Bristol Channel gives it the second-largest tidal range in the world; a tidal range (vertical difference between high tide and low tide) of up to 13m during springs can be experienced around Gower.

Big storms sitting offshore can affect these cliffs in two ways: first by creating a 'storm surge' effect which pushes the whole body of water further in than it would otherwise be, and second by creating big waves that dampen holds, moisten feet and wash your belayer off their ledge.

Even non-tidal venues can give you a soaking, Bowen's Parlour in a big swell.

Consider the following Top Tips to ensure you make the most of your day.

- Check before you go. Information about tide times and heights can be found online at www.climbers-club.co.uk/tides, or in a tide table bought in a local shop.
- Information in this guide is based on a rough average; what you experience on the day may not be what you were expecting.
- Pick your tide well. Spring tides offer more room at the crag's base at low water, but reach higher up the face at high tide. Neaps move less water around, allowing access to ledges all day on some crags (and preventing access to others).
- Keep an eye on the sea; it comes back in fast, especially in narrow zawns where it's funnelled in.
- Some waves team up out at sea to make rogue waves whose aim in life is to surprise and soak the unwary. Consider building a belay at the base of the cliff to avoid being swept away.

## VISITING GOWER

Below are some suggestions for places to eat, sleep and be merry when staying in the area; see the map on the inside cover for locations.

### ACCOMMODATION

There are options for all budgets when staying in the area, from camping to plush hotels. More information about all kinds of accommodation can be found by visiting www.the-gower.com.

Recommended campsites (see area map on the inside cover) include: (1) Pitton Cross near Rhossili; (2) Hillend at

Old iron lighthouse on north Gower coast. Photo: Wayne Tucker.

Llangennith; (3) Carreglwyd at Port Eynon; (4) Nicholaston Farm; and (5) Three Cliffs Bay. Wild camping is not allowed anywhere on Gower; please respect this and stay at a campsite.

Slightly further up the comfort scale is the Rhossili bunkhouse sleeping 22 people, ideal for individuals or groups. The YHA in Port Eynon (located in an old lifeboat house) is also a good option.

For those who prefer hotels, there are several on the peninsula as well as dozens in nearby Swansea. The Worm's Head Hotel at Rhossili is well situated at the western end of Gower and boasts stunning views.

## OUTDOOR SUPPLIES

The nearest Cotswold stores are in Llantrisant (just off the M4 J34 near Cardiff) or in Carmarthen, great if you realise you've forgotten something while *en route*. Climbing gear can be bought in Swansea High Street from Leisure Quest, or from Dynamic Rock climbing wall in Clydach. Various camping gear and outdoor supplies are available from Mike Davies Leisure in Upper Killay, just on the edge of Gower itself.

## CLIMBING WALLS

There are a few options for indoor climbing in South Wales, perfect for when the weather turns wet (which it has been known to do on occasion). The closest to Gower is Dynamic Rock in Clydach, just 2 minutes north of the M4 J45: a small friendly centre with good climbing and bouldering. Further west, Cardiff is home to Boulders: a large centre with a good range of walls, bouldering and training facilities.

## PUBS

There are many pubs in the area, but here is our pick of the bunch.

The Worm's Head Hotel at Rhossili has stunning views and is right next to the large car park.

The Countryman in Scurlage offers good reasonable food, beer and friendly local farmer types. Minibus runs to and from the Pitton Cross campsite are provided in the summer.

The King Arthur in Reynoldston has a popular beer garden and excellent cuisine.

The Kings Head in Llangennith is worth a visit if you're staying out that way, and very close to the popular surfing beach.

The Gower Inn is conveniently located on the main road in Parkmill. Its ample parking, seating and beer garden are good reasons to pay it a visit.

The Beaufort Arms in Kittle does a good pint and very good food.

The Joiners in Bishopston has great local beers and a friendly atmosphere (well worth a visit on the way home).

## FOOD

There are supermarkets in Swansea, Killay and Mumbles and small shops at Scurlage, Knelston, Parkmill and Southgate that should sort out lunch. However, you'd be foolish not to call into the Kittle Bakery and sample the best sandwiches, pasties and cakes in the area! For dinner there are the usual options of pub food, fish and chips in Scurlage and Mumbles and hundreds of restaurants of every kind in Swansea itself.

## OTHER ACTIVITIES

It's not just climbing on offer in this area: surfing, walking, mountain biking are all also available, as well as some world-class beaches for relaxing and family days out. If you're looking for the surf then the beaches of Llangennith, Rhossili, Caswell and Langland are popular spots, so it's worth bringing your board (although you can hire at some spots).

The National Trust provide some great walking maps of the area from their shop at Rhossili, showcasing the best the area has to offer. A walk onto Worms Head is highly recommended but be warned: the causeway is tidal and getting stuck on The Worm is a job for the lifeboat crews. Mountain biking on Gower is of limited appeal, but some good trails can be found. Just to the east is the Afan Forest Park, home to five world-class trails and some of the best Britain has to offer.

Stuart Llewellyn on the first ascent of *Pillars of the Earth* (F6b). Photo: Matt Woodfield.

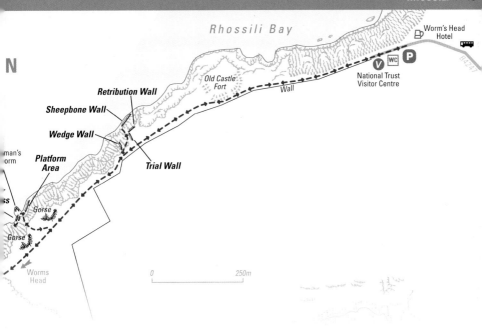

*Rhossili Bay*

N

Worm's Head
Hotel

Old Castle
Fort

Wall

Retribution Wall

Sheepbone Wall

Wedge Wall

National Trust
Visitor Centre

V WC P

man's
orm

Platform
Area

Trial Wall

s

Gorse

Gorse

Worms
Head

0          250m

# RHOSSILI

The cliffs of Rhossili overlook three miles of sandy beach, complete with ship wreck and haunted house. The crags are old quarried faces with a fine mix of both bolted and traditionally protected lines, as well as ample opportunity for deepwater soloing. If this isn't enough for you, then the car park is outside a pub, the walk in is flat and the sunsets are world class.

**Trial Wall:** After 5 minutes or so, when the track is closest to the cliff top edge, peel off and follow a path down to the right. The crag appears in front of you as you descend (the path is not as steep as it looks).

**Retribution Wall:** Found just around the corner from Trial Wall, follow the path down and around to the right.

**Wedge Wall:** This crag forms the bank of the descent path to Trial Wall. Head down as for Trial Wall and, as the main path heads right, peel off left and continue down a gully that leads to the base of the wall.

**Sheepbone Wall:** Located at sea level directly below Trial Wall. Head down to some ledges under Trial Wall, then either scramble down to beach level over more

ledges heading to the right, or make a short abseil down one of the corners to ledges below.

**Platform Area:** From where the drystone wall turns away from the track, head towards The Worm for another 100m until a path can be followed between two large gorse patches and down over a steep edge to the lower level. Below you is a large tidal platform frequented by fishermen. The crag is to the right of this and can be easily viewed on the approach. Scramble down ledges to reach the start of the routes.

**Poser Buttress:** As for Platform Area to the lower level, then follow the path to the left. The crag is tucked away in the narrow zawn below you.

☐ An aerial view of The Worm.
Photo: Wayne Tucker.

**Access agreements:** No climbing is allowed on Worms Head itself due to its international importance as a bird nesting site. The Head is home to many cliff-nesting birds including razorbills and the last colony of kittiwakes found in the area. There is also a breeding seal colony, another reason why Worms Head is a National Nature Reserve and Special Area of Conservation. Please respect this agreement, and the wildlife it protects.

The name 'Worms Head' comes from the Norse word 'Verm', meaning sea monster! It was given by passing Vikings who saw the waves breaking on the head and assumed this to be the serpent breathing fire and stayed well away… or so the story goes.

# TRIAL WALL

Trial Wall is an old west-facing quarry which offers good-quality steep rock and a mixture of both sport and traditional routes. The sheltered face dries quickly and gets the sun from about midday, making it an ideal location even on a winter afternoon.
SS 4066 8783
**Aspect:** W

**1 The Adulteress**      **24m E2 5c**
*FFA Andy Sharp & John Harwood 8th November 1981*

A beautiful line on the left side of the wall. Follow the crack energetically past the overhang, traverse right at the break and then keep it going up the final crack to finish.

**2 Blackman's Pinch**      **24m E4 6a**
*FFA Andy Sharp & John Harwood 5th December 1981*

The lower crack and overlap have some bolts, but you get to place your own gear for the finish shared with *The Adulteress.*

**3 Skull Attack**      **24m F7c**

*FFA Andy Sharp & Pete Lewis 15th April 1984*

Superb climbing up the technical wall. Head up to and past the overlap, then continue up past a thin break to a hard section that leads to the prominent groove.

**4 Crime and Punishment**      **23m E4 6b**

*FFA Andy Sharp & John Harwood 18th October 1981*

One of the stand-out routes of the crag and the first of the old aid routes to be freed here. Several bolts are in place, but a few wires are still needed for the sustained upper wall.

**5 Black Wall**      **23m F8a+**

*FA A. Forster & Andy Sharp 1988*

A thin start gains a thin crack, then awkward moves through the bulge lead to a desperate finish through the overhang. The original finish avoided the crux with a short traverse right, reducing the grade to a mere F7b+ (which makes for a more consistent and worthwhile outing in its own right).

**6 Inch Pinch**      **16m E3 6b**

*FA Andy Sharp & Pete Lewis 29th May 1983*

A hard bouldery start leads to easier climbing past the break of *Shakeout*.

**7 The Hant**      **16m F7a**

*FA Andy Sharp & Pete Lewis April 1987*

A right-hand variant to *Inch Pinch*, with good independent climbing in the upper section.

**8 Tribulations**      **12m F7a**

*FA Roy Thomas 20th September 1998*

The arête on the right provides complex off-balance moves.

**9 Shakeout**      **30m E3 5c**

*FA Andy Sharp & John Harwood 23rd October 1982*

A girdle of Trial Wall starting on the right and following the obvious break line to finish as for *The Adulteress*.

 Sabine Eggert on *Blackman's Pinch* (E4 6a).
Photo: Stefan Doerr.

# RETRIBUTION WALL

Retribution Wall is the seaward face just around the corner from Trial Wall, which offers a good mix of routes, styles and grades. The older traditional lines can now finish at the lower-offs, saving you the esoteric grassy finishes. This crag is not affected by the tide, but faces north and takes its time to dry outside of the summer months.

SS 4067 8785

**Aspect:** N

### ① Spades of Glory      16m F5+

*FA Matt Woodfield 21st August 2011*

Scramble up grassy ledges to gain the corner on the left side of the crag. Climb the corner using holds on the face on the right until a tricky step can be made to the lower-off.

### ② Laughing Spam Fritter      25m VS 4b

*FA Tony Penning & Peter Cresswell 8th November 1981*

Scramble precariously up to the base of the crack, layback up this before reaching the ramp and continue along the crack, stepping right at its end to gain the lower-off.

### ③ Pillars of the Earth      23m F6b

*FA Stuart Llewellyn 21st August 2011*

Climb the pillar of rock past the bulge and onto the slab above, avoiding the jug flakes out left (*Laughing Spam Fritter*). At the top move right to the lower-off.

### ③a World Without End      23m F6b

*FA Stuart Llewellyn 21st August 2011*

A variation on *Pillars of the Earth* approaches the difficult slab from the left side of the pillar over the roof.

### 4  Somme Mothers                                    23m HVS 5a
*FA Andy Sharp & John Harwood 8th November 1981*

Scramble to the base of the obvious crack and climb this
with interest to the lower-off.

### 5  24,000 Ballpoint Pens                            24m HS 4a
*FA Steve Warrington 21st August 2011*

Begin as for *Somme Mothers*, but follow the ledges right
to gain and climb the steep crack. Follow the crack above
to reach the lower-off.

### 6  Buckets of Bubbly                                25m  F5
*FA Steve Warrington 21st August 2011*

A technical start on small holds leads to an inconsiderate
ledge, mantel onto this and have a picnic. Move through
the stepped ramps and slab to the steep upper crack,
stepping left (crux) to reach the lower-off.

The wreck of the Helvetia.
Photo: Wayne Tucker.

# WEDGE WALL

Wedge Wall is a recent addition to the area and this small crag boasts several easy lines on quarried rock. It faces west and is quite sheltered, but feels very greasy when the rock is damp.

SS 4063 8781

**Aspect:** W

Matt Woodfield on *Wedge Dew Bin* (F5).
Photo: Stuart Llewellyn.

### ① The Fin End of the Wedge　　　　9m F5
*FA Stuart Llewellyn 9th September 2011*

The left-hand route up the positive arête starts with a tricky couple of moves out left, finishing in the grassy bay above.

### ② Wedgling　　　　9m F5
*FA Stuart Llewellyn 9th September 2011*

Go up the wall on good holds between ledges. At the top a hand traverse right (crux) leads to the lower-off.

### ③ Wedge-egade Master　　　　9m F5+
*FA Stuart Llewellyn 9th September 2011*

Brilliant wall climbing up the centre of the face.

### ④ Wedge Dew Bin　　　　8m F5
*FA Matt Woodfield 9th September 2011*

Good wall climbing on positive holds.

### ⑤ Atomic Wedgie　　　　8m F6a
*FA Matt Woodfield 9th September 2011*

Follow holds, both large and small, up the face.

# SHEEPBONE WALL

Sheepbone Wall is a sea-level crag with good rock and good low-grade routes; this overlooked and underrated venue is well worth a visit. Although not the tallest of crags, this venue does offer a real sea cliff feel.

When looking down the crag from below Retribution Wall, an oval pool can be seen at the base of *Chimney Crack* (a useful landmark when abseiling in). Climbing is possible from the ledges about 2 hours either side of low tide. The crag faces northwest so gets very little sun, making it slow to dry outside the summer months.

SS 4064 8785

**Aspect:** NW

**1 First Diedre** 10m D

*FA Jeremy Talbot 1968*

Head up the pitted wall and finish up the groove above.

**2 Mauk Wall** 10m S 4a

*FA Jeremy Talbot 1968*

A good route up the steep wall, passing the block on its left.

**3 Curving Crack** 10m HS 4b

*FA Jeremy Talbot 1968*

Climb to and along the obvious curving crack, gained from the deep cleft on the right. A bold direct start adds a grade.

**4 Chimney Crack** 10m VD

*FA Jeremy Talbot 1968*

Start in the corner and head up the chimney.

**5 Skull** 10m 4a HS

*FA Jeremy Talbot 1968*

Start as for *Chimney Crack*, then step right to the sloping ledge at 4m and climb the steep cracked wall above.

**6 Cross** 12m D

*FA Jeremy Talbot 1968*

Follow *Chimney Crack* to the ledge at 4m, then step right to finish up the easy groove.

**7 Deep Cut** 18m VD

*FA Jeremy Talbot 1968*

Gain the deep crack high on the wall by traversing in from the start of *Cross*. An alternative and steep direct start is rated severe.

**8 Forgotten Elephant**      14m HS 4b

*FRA Matt Woodfield & Stuart Llewellyn 19th April 2011*

The thin crack up the steep wall right of *Deep Cut* gained from below.

**9 Great Diedre**      12m S 4a

*FA Jeremy Talbot 1968*

The black slabby corner offers plenty of mediocre protection.

**10 Yellow Edge**      12m S

*FA Jeremy Talbot 1968*

Climb cracks right of the arête until a step left allows it to be followed to the top.

**11 Great Diedre II**      15m VS 4c

*FA C. Hard & Gwyn Evans 1975*

A good climb up the corner past a tricky overhang.

**12 Pistas Canute**      15m VS 4b

*FA Alun Beaton & Chris Allen 1989*

Start up *Slanting Chimney*, then break out leftwards up steep ground, around the arête and finish up the wall above.

**13 Slanting Chimney**      14m VD

*FA Mike Harber pre-1978*

Climb the slanting crackline.

**14 Gambolling Gareth's Arête**      17m E1 5a

*FA Alan Richardson & R. Lloyd 1992*

The arête is gained from the right and has a bold feel.

**15 Recess Crack**      17m VS 4c

*FA Jeremy Talbot 1968*

Head up the back of the recessed area then the top crack to finish.

# PLATFORM AREA

Platform Area is a quality venue set just above high tide level, sporting two good traditional routes and a fine deepwater solo.

SS 4038 8765

**Aspect:** NW

**1 Stardust**      24m HS 4a

*FA Andy Sharp & John Harwood 18th October 1981*

Drop down the groove from the platform and traverse left along the break until a move past an overlap (just before the arête) leads you up the final wall, taking care with the rock to finish.

**2 Year of the Snail**      24m VS 4b

*FA Matt Ward 16th August 1987*

Start as for *Stardust* but then head directly up the wall.

**3 Avoid Meeting the Portuguese Man-of-War** 40m VS 4c

*FA L. Davies & Phil Thomas July 1989*

A great deepwater solo with many variations and extensions. Start as for *Stardust* and continue around the arête, through the cave and into the sea on the other side, finishing up on easy rock across the water.

For a longer outing start on the pedestal next to the fishermen's platform, down climb the chimney and traverse around left to join the original route. Instead of jumping in at the end, make the tricky move around the next corner and keep moving left until you run out of rock, water, strength or sunlight. Lots of escape routes are available en route, as well as ledges to rest on.

> **WARNING**
>
> For any deepwater solo in this area a high tide is needed. Although most of the landings on this route are deep and clear of obstacles, some rocks do protrude below the water line and should be treated with caution. Check the landing zone at low water before attempting the route. Rough seas, water temperature, strong currents, other water users and seals should also be taken into account before setting off. If in doubt about the risks involved, don't do it.

# POSER BUTTRESS

The vertical wall of Poser Buttress houses a fine selection of crackline challenges above the sea. The square-cut zawn is very tidal, but the routes described are best started from the ledge belay marked on the topo (reached via abseil). Climbs can be started from the base about 1 hour either side of low water, but the lower wall takes time to dry and is not very pleasant. A hanging belay can be taken below any route, although this can be very uncomfortable. All routes can be viewed by scrambling round to a ledge on the other side of the zawn. The angle of the wall and the depth of water below at high tide means that these routes could be approached as deepwater solos.

SS 4934 8761

**Aspect:** NW

### 1 Normal Service 18m VS 4b

*FA Andy Sharp & John Harwood 5th December 1981*

From the belay ledge, climb right for a couple of metres and head up the first crack.

### 2 Splash Landing 20m HVS 5a

*FA Andy Sharp & John Harwood 5th December 1981*

Traverse right from the belay ledge and climb the second crack.

### 3 Dicky Five Stones 22m E3 5c

*FA Andy Sharp & Pete Lewis 1990*

A bold route that heads up the blank-looking wall between the cracks. Traverse in from the belay ledge and make technical moves with some long reaches up the wall. Climbing eases with height.

### 4 The Poser 24m E1 5b

*FA Tony Penning & Andy Sharp 23rd May 1982*

The third crack along is the best of the bunch, gained by a long traverse in from the belay ledge across a thin break.

### 5 Burning Rubber 26m E2 5b

*FA Tony Penning & Andy Sharp 23rd May 1982*

The final crack needs a long traverse to reach. Finish direct where the crack peters out.

Climbers enjoying *South West Diedre* (HVS 5a). Photo: Stuart Llewellyn.

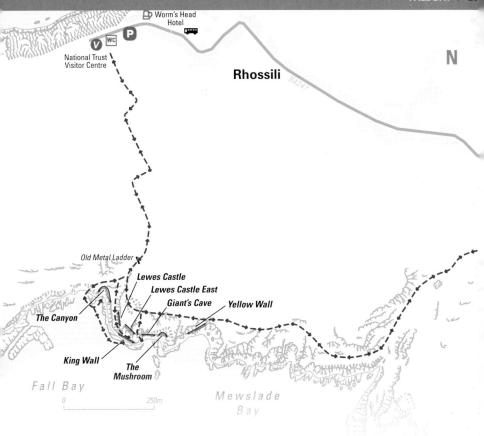

Worm's Head Hotel

National Trust
Visitor Centre

Rhossili

B4247

N

Old Metal Ladder

**Lewes Castle**
**Lewes Castle East**
**Giant's Cave**   **Yellow Wall**

**The Canyon**

**King Wall**
         **The**
         **Mushroom**

*Fall Bay*

0                250m

*Mewslade*
*Bay*

# FALL BAY

This area contains some of the best climbing on Gower. It's often visited and always loved. With more rock than you can shake a #7 nut at, this area has something for every climber from well-protected Diffs to steep, technical multi-pitch test pieces. You won't be disappointed.

The crags are split into an upper non-tidal tier and a lower tier rising straight out of the sand. The upper tier crags dry quickly and suffer little seepage. The lower crags can be slow to dry below the high water line on cloudy still days, and can be greasy in the heat. The crags face southeast–southwest so there's always something facing the sun; whether it's shining or not is another matter.

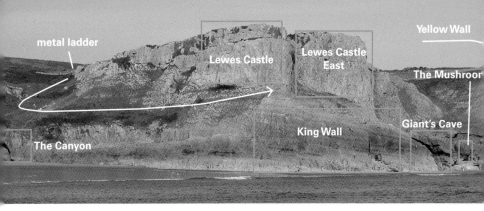

**Approach:** This area is best approached from the car park at Rhossili, where a small charge is payable. The crags can be reached in about 10 minutes from here. From the bottom of the main car park head left (south) away from the public toilets and follow a path that leads to a track. Turn right along this and enter the next field on the left. Follow this footpath through the next three fields over stiles towards the rocky headland until an old metal ladder is encountered alongside a newer set of wooden steps, looking down onto Fall Bay itself. From here the path splits.

**The Canyon:** Walk down the grassy slope and follow the path rightwards through an eroded trench that leads you onto the beach. Head left when you reach the sand. The crag is about 50m away directly beneath the descent path.

**Lewes Castle and Lewes Castle East:** These are the first of the upper tier crags. Head down the grassy slope and follow the narrow, worn track around to the left; Lewes Castle appears above you. Continue around the exposed corner and you'll find Lewes Castle East.

**King Wall:** If the tide is out then head down the grassy slope and follow the path rightwards through a trench that takes you onto the beach. Head across the sand and left around the corner to reach the base of the crag. Alternatively, use the Lewes Castle approach to the large gearing-up ledge (the Great Terrace). Depending on the tide, either abseil from here or walk off down the rocky slope to the beach and around the corner to arrive at the base of the crag.

**Giant's Cave:** From the metal ladder head left along the cliff-top path and scramble down the first gully on the far side of the headland. Giant's Cave appears on your left and can't be missed: just look for a cave that's, well… giant.

**Yellow Wall:** From the metal ladder, head left along the cliff-top path passing the first bay containing Giant's Cave until above the Great Boulder Cove. Yellow Wall forms the western side of this cove and can be accessed by abseil or by carefully scrambling down the steep ground on the east side of the cove.

# THE CANYON

A steep sheltered zawn in the back of Fall Bay offers some good bouldering straight off the sand. The rock is solid down low but can be fragile near the top, worth noting if you start doing highball problems. The base is washed clean on spring tides and stays dry on neaps, giving a reliable spot to warm up, finish your day or just potter about while the BBQ warms up.

There are a variety of straight-up problems, as well as an entertaining traverse of the entire zawn which is varied and interesting.

SS 4136 8737

**Aspect**: E, S and W

# LEWES CASTLE

This buttress overlooks Fall Bay itself and has more than its fair share of classic lines. Set well above the sea, it offers quality non-tidal routes that are so beautifully positioned that it's worth breaking some routes into two pitches just to enjoy gazing down across the water; just don't forget to keep belaying! The top is often breezy and the capping overhangs can prevent easy communication between the cliff top and base.

SS 4140 8727

**Aspect**: SW

Although a flagship of traditional climbing in the area, some of the evidence suggests a less traditional approach to ascents on the buttress. Keep your eyes open for old bolt holes (*Rhea*, etc.), aid pegs (*Lazy Sunday Aternoon*, etc.) and a fully cemented belay cave (*Isis*).

 **Ket**      **34m HVS 5b**

*FA Eryl Pardoe & Richard Leigh 1967*

The initial corner crack has a hard move, the middle a rest near a small cave and the finish an interesting fight through an ivy patch. Alternatively, climb direct up the crack (same grade).

**❷ Seket**      **34m E1 5b**

*FA Eryl Pardoe & Alan March 1968*

Climb the groove and then a slab past the overhang to a crack in the right wall, then to the top. Most of the protection relies on pegs and other old gear.

**❸ Monkey See and Monkey Do**    **34m E3 5c**

*FA Andy Sharp & Pete Lewis 17th February 2002*

Climb a vague groove with an old peg at 5m. Boldly surmount the overlap (Friend 4!), move up (peg) through the final overlap (thread) and finish easily rightwards.

**❹ Reptiles and Samurai**      **34m E4 6a**

*FA Martin Crocker & Matt Ward 28th June 1987*

A good route with a serious start. Climb up to and over a bulge (good runner) to a short groove, move upwards past old pegs to and over the roof. Finish up the groove on the left.

Chris Allan Jr bouldering in The Canyon
Photo: Rockall Images

**5 Isis**       **36m HVS 5a**

*FA Robert Griffiths & Eryl Pardoe February 1967*

A fantastic and popular line that will require your big nuts. Follow the obvious central crack of the crag to the overhang above. Traverse right towards a small cave and pull through the overhang to finish leftwards.

**6 Horus**       **34m HVS 5a**

*FA Peter Hinder & Jeremy Talbot 1975*

Climb the right-hand crack past an old peg to step left onto a small pinnacle. Move up to the break and finish as for *Isis*.

**7 Rhea**       **34m HVS 5a**

*FA Richard Leigh & Trevor Smith 1967*

Start below the left side of the large overhang and head up past a recess to gain a groove. Move right and head for the V groove on the left edge of the overhang above.

**8 Osiris**       **36m VS 4c**

*FA Eryl Pardoe & Robert Griffiths 1967*

Follow the grooves to the widest part of the overhang (optional stunning belay). Hand traverse rightwards on polished holds under the roof (clipping the ancient wooden wedge for luck), pass the overhang at its weakest point and finish direct.

**9 Lazy Sunday Afternoon**       **34m E2 5b**

*FA Gary Lewis & Steve Mundy 1982*

A one-move wonder, but a good wander. Best done by following *Osiris* to the traverse, then break out through the widest point of the roof past a good thread and an old peg to finish up easier ground.

**10 Seth**       **34m E1 5c**

*FA Jeremy Talbot 1970*

Very hard (but not for long), this climb is at the top end of the grade. Start as for *Osiris*, then head up the steep crack on the right wall past a hard move or two to rejoin *Osiris* through the roof. Alternatively, from the top of the crack traverse left to the big roof and finish as for *Lazy Sunday Afternoon* to give for a more sustained finish.

**11 Horsis**       **34m HVS 5a**

*FA Eryl Pardoe & Robert Griffiths 1968*

From the bottom of *Osiris* head right into a groove. Follow cracks passing a large block to finish easily in a groove right of the overhang.

# LEWES CASTLE EAST

This is the next buttress around the corner from Lewes Castle at the same level, containing a couple of low-grade routes as well as the fantastic *South West Diedre*. Routes that pass through the cave area are not recommended in the nesting season due to angry fulmars and their foul-smelling projectiles.

SS 4143 8727

**Aspect**: S

The grassy top of Lewes Castle is marked with the circular ditch-and-bank remains of an Iron Age hill fort, a scheduled ancient monument. These settlements were topped with a defensive wooden wall to protect the inhabitants of the period between when hunter-gatherers dwelled in the local caves and the foundation of the villages that we know today. Similar remains can be seen at Third Sister and Thurba Head to the east, and on the approach to the Rhossili crags.

### ① Gethsemane 26m S 4a

*FA South Wales Mountaineering Club 1966*

Start on the grassy slope on the left side of the buttress, and gain the ledge above by a rising traverse from the left. Follow the grooves above, taking care with the rock in the final section.

### ② Eden 26m HS 4b

*FA Jeremy Talbot 1971*

Climb the groove, taking care with the rock in places, to the small overhang. Traverse left and finish up the rib above. Alternatively, traverse right to join the final section of *The Bottle* (VS 4c) for a more interesting finish.

### ③ The Bottle 27m VS 4c

*FA Jeremy Talbot & Peter Hinder 1974*

Climb into the cave, avoiding any angry seagulls that may be nesting along the way. Step left and surmount the pedestal, finish steeply up the cracks above.

### ④ Cave Cracks 32m E2 5c

*FA Pat Littlejohn & Alan Davies 18th March 1980*

From the cave of *The Bottle*, climb the right wall until it is possible to step left and gain the jams in the roof above. Struggle up past this to finish up the steep wall on obvious cracks.

### ⑤ South West Diedre 28m HVS 5a

*FA Swansea University Mountaineering Club 1967*

A classic route that has become a rite of passage. Climb the corner and groove to a halfway ledge. Step round left and head up past a small overhang to finish steeply on good holds. If you bottle the hard moves, it is possible go rightwards from the halfway ledge up the wide corner crack, reducing the grade to VS 4c.

**Instigator**                 28m HVS 5a

*FA John Kerry & Martyn Hogge 1969*

A bold start and lovely finish. Climb a crack then a groove to a recess, finish up the rib or rightwards across the smooth wall.

 **Combination**                 44m VS 4b

*FA Jeremy Talbot & Peter Hinder 1973*

Follow the blocky loose-feeling groove to the break, traverse left to and around the arête, then finish up the wide corner crack above. Careful ropework will prevent immobilising drag.

**8** **South East Arête**                 33m E3 5c

*FA Martin Crocker & John Harwood 24th April 1999*

Take the narrow left-facing corner on the front of the buttress and follow easier ground to a horizontal break. Move up the head wall on small pockets and friction moves to the arête and finish.

# KING WALL

King Wall is the tidal crag below Lewes Castle; it is slabby, solid and a great playground for the gentler grades. The rock starts from the sand and ends on the Great Terrace, the large ledge that separates King Wall from Lewes Castle East. The crag is split in the middle by the large crack of *Great Cleft* and indented by the square-cut recess of *Odin* to the east. As a guide, it is accessible 2 hours 30 mins either side of low water. That being said, sometimes (on neap tides) the sea doesn't leave the base of the crag. Fear not however as you can abseil off the large block down to ledges above the sea on most routes, creating a beautiful situation. Just watch out for big waves! Descent is easiest by walking right (facing inland) and scrambling down to beach level near Giant's Cave.

SS 4139 8726

**Aspect**: S

Roy Thomas contemplating the next moves on *Instigator* (HVS 5a). Photo: Carl Ryan.

The Great Terrace

Abseil
(large block)
↓

### ① Frigg                                      27m VS 4b

*FA Jeremy Talbot & David Lewis 1963*

A good route, but does not dry out after rain as fast as other routes on the face. Start at the bottom of the left hand of two grooves in the wall. Follow the groove, moving left when it runs out, to finish on the Great Terrace. Belay well back.

### ② Ragnarok                                   29m HS 4a

*FA Jeremy Talbot & David Lewis 1963*

An absorbing route with good climbing. Climb the rightward-trending groove past a stained overlap high up.

### ③ Sweyn                                       29m HS 4b

*FA Jeremy Talbot & David Lewis 1963*

Follow the white calcite streaks, then finish direct.

### ④ King Route                                    21m S

*FA Derrick Jones & Jeremy Talbot 1959*

The original route of the crag. Move up the left side of the pillar, following ledges rightwards to finish.

### ⑤ Great Cleft                                   21m D

*FA Jeremy Talbot & Derrick Jones 1959*

The obvious crack splitting the crag in two. Can be used as a descent, but be warned: it is polished in places.

### ⑥ Balder                                      21m VS 5a

*FA Jeremy Talbot 1963*

Balance up the slab on small holds and small gear. Can be greasy in warm weather.

### ⑦ Fafnir                                       21m HS 4b

*FA Jeremy Talbot 1963*

Head up the corner, stepping boldly left under the overhang to finish.

### ⑧ Amble                                         21m VD

*FA Jeremy Talbot 1961*

This slabby route follows the cracked wall and is very pleasant.

### ⑨ Pytt                                           21m S

*FA Jeremy Talbot 1962*

Straight up the pitted wall.

### ⑩ Odin                                         21m VS 4b

*FA Jeremy Talbot 1963*

Comes with a traditional feel. The smooth chimney narrows to a crack where being small is an advantage.

### ⑪ Needle Crack                                21m VS 4b

*FA Jeremy Talbot 1963*

Climb the steep corner to easier ground, then up the final steep section.

# GIANT'S CAVE

A playground for the strong and the brave, this huge cave sports horizontal roof moves, exposed traverses and a "preposterous" exit through a blowhole (which works just as well as an exciting abseil entry for those so inclined). Routes starting from the sand are accessible around 3 hours either side of low water. *Nick'd* and routes to the left of *Masterpiece* are non-tidal, but will be affected by big seas.

SS 4149 8726

**Aspect**: E, S, W

### ① Red Admiral    13m E3 6a
*FA Andy Sharp & Pete Lewis 1984*

The arête to the left of the cave.

### ② Errant    14m E2 5c
*FA Jeremy Talbot & Beryl Talbot 1965*

A little gem, lost in the shadow of its mighty neighbours. The fierce technical corner: traverse left to a belay.

### ③ Masterpiece    31m E6 6b
*FA Pat Littlejohn & Malcolm Campbell 13th May 1984*

The arête is steep, technical and downright hard. Gain

the arête from either side. Progress using pockets at first, then flat holds higher up. Hard moves then lead to the break. Finish up the groove and rock above.

### ④ Thriller    31m E4 6a
*FFA Pat Littlejohn & Chris Hurley 2nd May 1984*

A striking line starting up the wide crack just inside the left wall of the cave. Burst across under the roof, along a strenuous traverse to exit up the hanging corner.

> This is one of many former aid routes freed by Pat Littlejohn, originally climbed by Jeremy Talbot and named Twm Shon Catti (after the legend of Welsh folklore).

### ⑤ A Rush of Blood to the Head    31m E6 6b
*FA Martyn Richards & Andy Sharp 2001*

As for *Thriller* to the traverse, then move out across the roof to a large crack. Tackle the hanging groove to finish.

### ⑥ Can't Buy a Thrill    31m E5 6b
*FA Andy Sharp & Pete Lewis 1986*

A calm approach, good use of your feet and a refined jamming technique are required. As for *Thriller* to the traverse, then explode out along the roof on big holds. Turn the lip and finish rightwards up the front face of the cave.

### 7 The Divine Guiding Light
36m E6 6b

*FA Martin Crocker & Matt Ward 16th August 1987*

Head up cracks on the steep left wall of the cave passing a rotten peg. Follow good jams towards the light and bridge up the blowhole to exit. Calm sea and cool breeze desirable.

### 8 Charlie Don't Surf
18m E4 6a

*FA Andy Sharp & Owen Jones 1986*

A tricky start leads to a sloping ledge at the high water line. Pull onto the leaning wall and finish leftwards up the steep corner on better holds. Low in the grade, the bouldery start is avoided when the sea covers it.

### 9 Madame Butterfly
18m E5 6b

*FFA Andy Sharp & Pete Lewis 1984*

Reliant on rusty old pegs for the traditional lead, but well suited to deepwater solo with the steep barnacled start being underwater. From the sand, head up barnacled rock and the crack to the wide fissure at the high water line. Climb the steep wall above that leads to and around the overhang, finishing direct.

### 10 Nick'd
40m E2 5b

*FA Adrian Wilson & Eamon Kellar 1990*

An airy traverse along the wall above the lip of the cave. For a little extra excitement wait for high tide and some big waves. Start from a ledge above the right side of the cave, from which easy climbing leads to a puzzling section. Keep heading left, passing the groove with the final difficulty, to belay above the corner of *Errant*.

### 11 Shannara
15m HS 4a

*FA P. Hornsby & S. Hornsby 1978*

Gain and climb the arête from the right.

### 12 Sham
15m D

*FA Jeremy Talbot 1960*

Climb the middle of the wall, moving right to finish up the groove.

To the east of Giant's Cave is a large flake of rock with steep walls. This is The Mushroom, which provides a good traverse on its eastern face. It is best climbed solo with the sea lapping at your feet.

### 13 Flake
12m HS 4a

*FA Jeremy Talbot & Beryl Talbot 1965*

Start on the top of the flake, drop down the corner and traverse on good sharp holds leftwards along the obvious curving line. Either finish direct up the wall or continue traversing around into Giant's Cave and link into another route.

⬛ Charles Romijn trying not to take the plunge from *Madame Butterfly* (E5 6b), Giant's Cave. Photo: Stuart Llewellyn.

# YELLOW WALL

Some of the best steep rock and hard routes on Gower are found on Yellow Wall, almost as if the crag has escaped from its bigger brothers in Pembroke. It yields fantastic rewards for those who brave the free-hanging abseil into Great Boulder Cove, an area with little option for escape. On a first visit, it would be well worth walking around to the top of the other side of the cove to get a good look at the lines before heading down. The crag is tidal and accessible around 3 hours either side of low tide.

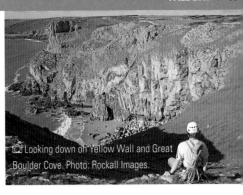
Looking down on Yellow Wall and Great Boulder Cove. Photo: Rockall Images.

Many of the routes are equipped with pegs for protection. However, these were most likely placed on the first ascent and will now be of questionable quality.

There are a couple of ways to access the bottom of the crag. You can make a long abseil in via stakes or from rock further back, or scramble down and around the east side of the cove. To escape from Boulder Cove you can scramble steeply up the east side (right when facing inland) on rock and grass. Alternatively, on a low spring tide you can just walk away. If all else fails, break out your prusiks and head back up your abseil line.

You don't have to abseil in with this big book stuffed down your top. A free download of Yellow Wall is available online from the publishers Pesda Press (www.pesdapress.com). Print it out and there's your perfect pocket-sized guide.

**Access agreements**: A seasonal restriction is in place due to nesting birds from 1st March to 15th August; no climbing is allowed on Yellow Wall during this period. This restriction is reviewed in May and lifted if nesting is completed early. For more information and updates, see the BMC's Regional Access Database.

For the first couple of routes it is best to abseil down the line indicated, allowing you to use the rope to belay and assist the grassy scramble to the top.

SS 4160 8727
**Aspect**: SE

THIS ONE'S GOING IN MILES!

Charles Romijn.

### 1 Winter Warmer                    24m E3 6a

*FA Mick Learoyd & Roy Thomas 1985*

Boulder through the bulge via a crack. Climb through the shallow groove systems, branch off left and finish by your pre-placed rope.

### 2 Skylark                          40m E2 5c

*FA Chris King & Steve Monks 1978*

Climb to the overhang at 4m, take it on its left-hand side, then bear right into the clean-cut corner. Continue up this to a ledge, before finishing up a crack in the steep wall.

### 3 Muppet Show                      40m E1 5a

*FA Andy Sharp 1976*

A classic introduction to this wall. Head up the corner to a large ledge before moving out left under an arête. Layback the flake towards the break and traverse this leftwards. Bridge the exposed corner and continue to easier ground, belaying by your pre-placed rope. *Skylark* makes for a pleasant alternative finish.

### 4 Enigma                           40m E4 6b

*FFA Pat Littlejohn & Steve Lewis 28th November 1982*

Follow *Muppet Show* for a few metres until a line of undercuts draws you left past an overhang and up the groove above. When the holds run out, find sloping ones on the arête to the left. Follow this with care to the top.

### 5 Heroin                           49m E5 6b

*FA Martin Crocker & Matt Ward 31st August 1986*

**1. 25m 6a** Follow *Enigma* to the ledge in the groove.
**2. 12m 6b** Move out right across the wall past a couple of pegs and up the arête to a ledge.
**3. 12m 5b** Head up the arête, finishing left.

**6** **Yellow Wall** 45m E3 5c

*FFA Pat Littlejohn & Andy Houghton February 1972*

*The* route of the wall that takes the striking central groove.
**1. 33m 5c** Climb the first groove to the overhang. Make a
m ove left and admire the perfectly smooth bird runway
(possible belay here). Move diagonally rightwards past a
peg to the enticing corner, and go up this to belay on the
large ledge.
**2. 12m 5c** Boldly climb the corner at the back of the
ledge for a few metres before trending left to another
shallow corner, which is followed to the top.

**7** **Chasing the Dragon** 45m E8 6c

*FA Adrian Berry 2nd September 1999*

**1. 15m 5c** Climb as for *Yellow Wall*, taking a belay in
the cave.
**2. 30m 6c** Head diagonally rightwards to the base of the
groove then move left to the bottom of the wall, making
a long reach for a jug and peg. Powerful moves through
the wall gain the arête and finish of *Heroin*.

**8** **Steam Train** 45m E4 6a

*FA Andy Sharp & Pete Lewis 1985*

**1. 33m 6a** Climb a shallow groove to overhangs. Wander
right for 3m then move into another groove. Follow this
to the belay ledge.
**2. 12m 5b** Traverse round the arête to the right and onto
a red slab. Traverse across this to a groove, which is
climbed for 1m before swinging back left. Head up the
last short groove to finish.

In 1973 *Sea Cliff Climbing in Great Britain* was
published, stating that Yellow Wall had "the most
classical artificial climbing…". Pat Littlejohn had
freed the routes in question before the ink could dry,
starting an onslaught of excellent traditional routes
on the cliff.

**9** **Transformer** 48m E3 6a

*FFA Chris King & Steve Monks 1978*

**1. 27m 6a** The crux is getting around the lower roof. After
this follow the corner and rightward-slanting groove
before sweeping in left onto the belay ledge.

Nick Gillett on *Steam Train*
(E4 6a), lost in a sea of rock.
Photo: Charles Romijn

Simon Rawlinson protecting the last moves
of Yellow Wall's first pitch (E3 5c)
Photo: Stuart Llewellyn.

📷 Coasteering, Giant's Cave.
Photo: Stuart Llewellyn.

**2. 21m 5c** Move right into the groove system and pull through to the obvious deep crack on the right-hand wall. 'Beast' yourself up this to the finish.

### 🔟 Man of Yellow                          44m E6 6b

A combination of the better and safer pitches of *Man of the Earth* and *Yellow Regeneration*, offering some fantastic steep climbing. You'll be clipping some old pegs; good luck…
*FA P1 Gary Gibson & Roy Thomas 15th October 1989*

**1. 20m 6b** Begin up the slim groove and move rightwards across steep ground, moving back left to follow the line of old pegs and a thread through the overlaps. Belay from cracks in the wall at the break, or head a little higher and use the old peg belay.
*FA P2 Martin Crocker & Roy Thomas 30th August 1986*

**2. 24m 6b** Head up and across the wall to the arête on the right. This is followed (via a large thread) with a long reach to easier ground.

### 11 Skyhedral Wall                          40m E6 6b
*FA Martin Crocker 1991*

Large wires and medium cams will be useful on this long pitch, which has three good shakeouts and numerous old pegs. Climb the overhanging layback cracks before taking on the bulge. Head for the hand rail and a good rest. From this, head to a niche with good jugs then take a slim groove on the right before blasting through a bulge. Next you come across a leftward-facing groove to a horizontal break. Traverse your hands left, and pull over another bulge to a juggy break. Get into the small niche, gain a good break and head left to finish.

### 12 Holy Grail                          45m E2 5b
*FA Pat Littlejohn & John Harwood 3rd October 1980*

Not as hideous as it first appears, this route dares to head up the corner between the solid face and the broken choss at the back of the cove. Climb past the jutting block, heading left into the corner. Undercling left past the overhang to a lovely finish up the final corner/chimney.

Climbers enjoying a perfect day on *Kaiser* (HVS 5a 4c). Photo: Rockall Images.

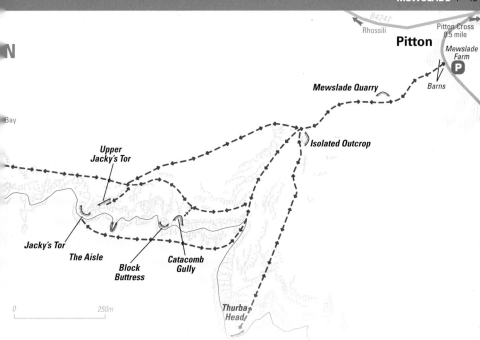

# MEWSLADE

With the tide out, Mewslade Bay is a huge expanse of beautiful sand stretching out past small caves and secluded zawns. With the tide in, the bay is reclaimed once more by the sea which engulfs the lower cliffs and reaches out to those above. The bay is bounded to the east by Thurba Head and to the west by Jacky's Tor. While there is a vast amount of rock between the two, only some of it is worth climbing. Some of the crags are at sea level and others are non-tidal, giving you options for climbing at any time.

**Approach**: About a mile before Rhossili, the hamlet of Pitton lies in the bottom of a valley. Follow signposts on the left for 'Mewslade Farm and Car Park', parking in a farmer's field, and putting some change in the honesty box. The path you need is opposite the car park between two old barns. Follow this through a short wood until a gate leads you into the open near Mewslade Quarry (slabby bouldering). Continue down the dry valley towards the sea, and from here follow the directions for individual crags below.

**Jacky's Tor:** Follow the path down the rocks and onto the beach. Head rightwards across the sand to the obvious headland with the detached pinnacles on its seaward end; this is Jacky's Tor. The Cave Area is reached by scrambling up round the left side of the Front Face, and the East Wall faces you as you approach.

**Upper Jacky's Tor:** Halfway down the dry valley is an isolated outcrop. From here turn right at the crossroads and head up the hill. Turn left at the top and follow the path until it meets the corner of a drystone wall and a

Upper Jacky's Tor

Block Buttress

Catacomb Gully

coastal path signpost. Head down towards the sea and 'The Aisle' (a long finger of rock). When you reach rocky ground follow a vague footpath to the right over broken terrain and up the grass slope to the base of the crag.

**Block Buttress:** Follow the path down the rocks and onto the beach, head right and Block Buttress is the first large headland you will reach.

**Catacomb Gully:** From the end of the valley, follow the coastal path round right until an eroded gully leads down to the top of Right Wall. Scramble down the rib in front of you to the bottom of the gully, then carefully cross the abyss. This point can also be reached by scrambling up from the beach just before Block Buttress.

**Thurba Head:** Halfway down the dry valley is an isolated outcrop. Follow a path through the gate on the left and up the hill to the top. Walk out seawards along the headland, then drop down to the other side following a worn path to a rocky ledge above the sea.

# MEWSLADE QUARRY

SS 4247 8753

**Aspect**: S

The clean slab of Mewslade Quarry has good landings, is sheltered, catches the early sun, dries remarkably fast after rain and suffers little seepage. Perfect for a warm-up or bouldering session, it is however frequented by outdoor centres, is a little polished at its base and lacks sustained technical interest. That said, it is still worth a visit if you're passing (even just for a quick explore in the small cave).

Thrift. Photo: Matt Woodfield.

Becky Bailey bouldering Mewslade Quarry. Photo: Matt Woodfield.

# JACKY'S TOR

This grand tor is home to Gower's earliest hard route and offers a selection of quality routes across the grades, from Diff to E6 and everything in between. The area is split into four sections, all worth a visit, but you'll want a low tide for the Front and East faces. Each area has its own style and character, and there is always somewhere to climb whatever the state of the tide.

## CAVE AREA

Solid rock and striking lines are found in the recessed area above the sand on the left side of the tor. The starts can also be reached by scrambling down with care from the west side of the tor when the tide prevents access from the beach. Approach as for Upper Jacky's Tor, but at the wall drop down the far side of the tor on steep grass then rock.

The routes start from the cave 10m above the beach, making them non-tidal.

SS 4167 8721

**Aspect**: S

 **Cave Corner**      **20m D**

*FA Unknown*

From the cave continue easily up the left wall through a groove to finish. Can be used as a descent.

**2 Chantilly Lace**      **21m HVS 5b**

*FA Andy Sharp & John Harwood 23rd October 1982*

A splendid corner climb, which will be a real test of your bridging capabilities. The corner has sinker gear and fine climbing the whole way, but the route is in no way a pushover.

**3 Shock and Awe**      **21m E6 6c**

*FA Martyn Richards & Andy Sharp 27th March 2003*

Awesome steep climbing through the centre of the cave passing three thread runners.

[O] Liz Collyer on the beautifully positioned *Cave Traverse* (HS 4a) Photo: Make The Next Move Images.

## FRONT FACE

The most seaward point on the tor has two excellent routes, but beware of the tide. The sea only clears the base on spring tides and sneaks back in with speed, offering up to 45 minutes either side of low water (so don't hang around). Descent from the top can either be made by abseil from a big thread, or rightwards along ledges from the tops. Top tip: don't leave your sack at the base unless it can float and you can swim.
SS 4168 8720
**Aspect**: S

**1 V Groove**                                       **27m E3 5c**

*FA Eryl Pardoe & Derek Ellis 1966*

An early technical route that brought E3 to Gower. Start directly below the V-shaped groove high on the front face; reach this via the rib and thin crack. Exit leftwards, head up cracks above to a ledge and then either abseil off the big thread or traverse off right with care.

**2 Plot 13**                                         **27m E4 6a**

*FA Roy Thomas, John Bullock & Len Moran 31st March 1987*

High in the grade, this line goes up the right side of the

**4 Possessed**                                       **22m E4 6a**

*FA Andy Sharp & John Harwood 30th October 1982*

Climb the flake crack on the right of the cave, step left from the small ledge and gain the thin crack running up the wall above. Protection is not great.

**5 Repossessed**                                     **22m E4 6a**

*FA Martyn Richards & Andy Sharp 27th March 2003*

Start as for *Possessed* but head up the steep groove above the small ledge to finish as for *Cave Traverse*.

**6 The Damned**                                      **22m E2 6a**

*FA Andy Sharp & Dennis Hillier 27th March 2003*

Start as for *Possessed* but head right and climb the crack above that leads past a small roof and becomes a steep corner. Traverse left to finish as for *Cave Traverse*.

**7 Cave Traverse**                                   **30m HS 4a**

*FA Roger Owen & Chris Andrews 1982*

Climb the steep right wall, then follow the corner above to a traverse line level with the top of the cave. Traverse boldly across the lip of the cave past two rusty pegs and a badly placed bush.

descent

front face. Begin up the steep chimney and struggle until it is possible to step out right. Head up the thin crack to the left towards the overhang; the hidden hold above is reached by a hard but protectable move. Further stiff climbing leads you up the headwall and to a ledge, then either abseil off the big thread or traverse off right with care.

## EAST FACE

Facing you on the approach across the beach, the East Wall offers good steep climbing off the beach to ledges near the upper cliff. A couple of good lines are found on this side of the tor; they share the same start and are worth seeking out. This area of the tor is less tidal than the front, being accessible about 1 hour 30 mins either side of low water.

SS 4171 8720

**Aspect**: SE

**③ Red Diedre**                 **18m HVS 5a**

*FA Jeremy Talbot & David Lewis 1963*

The obvious steep corner gained by easy rock offers good, well-protected climbing.

**④ Mittel**                      **18m VD**

*FA Jeremy Talbot & David Lewis 1963*

Start as for *Red Diedre* but finish up the arête to the right.

## UPPER JACKY'S TOR

A non-tidal crag that offers some beautifully situated mid-grade routes. Facing southeast it catches the morning sun and is often sheltered from the wind, making it a reliable location. In the middle of the face there is a 'shield' of rock, with a detached flake at the base directly below it.

Descent can be made by heading back inland to the stone wall then as for the approach, or go 20m further along the headland and down a rocky scramble (Mod) on the front edge of the tor, then follow the grassy ledges back to the base.

SS 4174 8723

**Aspect**: SE

**① Cod Piece**                 **23m HS 4b**

*FA Alan Beaton & Guy Richardson 1982*

A good entry-level climb for the HS grade. Follow the groove rightwards to a ledge, and step boldly rightwards from here in between good gear to the top of the 'shield'. Finish up the wall and left corner above, taking care with the rock.

**② Thanksgiving**            **22m HVS 5a**

*FA Pat Littlejohn 22nd November 1982*

Follow the groove leftwards past a ledge, continuing leftwards through the steepening groove to finish.

**③ Praise Be**                 **21m E1 5a**

*FA Martin Crocker 5th December 1998*

A bold undertaking; surmount the 2m high flake in the centre of the wall, step right off the top and climb direct up the centre of the shield above, finishing up the wall and right corner.

**④ Raindrops**      **21m HVS 5a**

*FA Gwyn Evans & Guy Richardson 1981*

A pleasant outing that starts below the shield of rock. Follow cracks rightwards for a couple of metres, then direct via good side pulls up the right side of the shield. Finish up the wall and steep right corner.

**⑤ All There**      **24m VS 4c**

*FA Gwyn Evans & John Bullock 1982*

And it is. Start below the shield of rock, follow a line of cracks and broken grooves rightwards until the rock steepens. Move right and break through the steep ground to find easier climbing above.

**⑥ A Bit On The Side**      **23m VS 4b**

*FA Guy Richardson & Mike Danford 1982*

Follow a rightward-trending broken crackline to below a small overhang. Traverse boldly under this and finish up the groove.

**⑦ A Day Out With Dave**      **23m HVS 5a**

*FA Tony Rees & Dave Phillips July 2006*

Just left of the small cave on the right of the crag is a pillar of rock. Climb this then the crack above to the slab below the small overhang. Fix good wires on the left, then follow the holds through the steep ground to easy rock above.

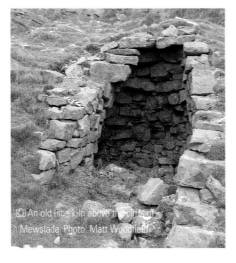
*An old lime kiln above the cliffs of Mewslade. Photo: Matt Woodfield.*

# BLOCK BUTTRESS

Block Buttress is an impressive crag rising straight out of the sand. The obvious red scar in its upper reaches represents the remains of a major rockfall in the 1990s. Washed smooth at its base, pitted rough in the spray zone and fragile on the top, this buttress has a bit of everything for your fingers to work on.

The sand level can change by several metres, making the routes longer and some starts trickier. Accessible about 2 hours either side of low water, the gully can stay wet and greasy in dull weather. The routes on either side dry quickly, however.

SS 4190 8716

**Aspect**: S

**① Southwest Edge**      **60m M**

*FA Jeremy Talbot & Richard Corbett 1962*

A worthwhile route taking the rib and easy ground above (possible as a descent for the next few routes).

**② Piz**      **12m HS 4b**

*FA Jeremy Talbot & Richard Corbett 1962*

The groove in the left wall, starting on the ledge above the sand and easing with height.

**③ Funny Fish In A Hole**      **21m E1 5c**

*FA N. Taylor 2nd August 1997*

The steep smooth crack in the left wall, starting near the back of the gully.

**④ Cima**      **36m E1 5b**

*FA Jeremy Talbot & Richard Corbett 1962*

The striking crackline up the back wall of the gully takes you past some tricky moves and into a niche. The crackline leads above this with continued interest to the top.

> The cave-like structures seen around the coast of Gower are lime kilns, used to heat the rock and create lime (a powder used as a fertiliser, mortar and plaster). The spiky gorse bushes that surround them were planted to fuel the fires as the plant burns hot and leaves little ash.

# CATACOMB GULLY

This gully is set well above the sea with east- and west-facing walls. This valuable non-tidal venue offers a range of grades, often with a choice of sun or shade, but little in the way of classics. Access is gained by either scrambling up from the beach or down the obvious path and rocky ridge from the cliff-top path. The rock at the top of Left Wall should be treated with care; old stakes are in place further back towards the footpath.

## LEFT WALL
SS 4193 8718

**Aspect**: SE

### ① Celtic Uprising      12m E1 5b
*FA Martin Crocker 1st August 1987*

Take a direct line using positive but small holds until flakes trend leftwards. Move rightwards to the pocket before finishing straight up.

### ② Relics      15m E3 6a
*FA Mick Learoyd & Haydn Griffiths 1986*

A brilliant technical line with little protection for the difficulties found in its bottom half. Pass the old un-clippable bolt to reach good holds in twin vertical slots. From here climb leftwards to finish as for *Celtic Uprising*, passing a worrying in situ thread on a peg.

### ③ West Corner Crack      15m HS 4b
*FA Jeremy Talbot & Richard Corbett 1961*

Follow the obvious crack in the corner that widens to a chimney further up. The difficult start can be avoided to the right.

### ④ Ribbery      15m S
*FA Jeremy Talbot & Richard Corbett 1961*

Pleasant climbing heading up the wall, keeping left of the arête.

### ⑤ Rib And Crack      15m HS 4a
*FA Jeremy Talbot & Richard Corbett 1961*

An inviting corner crack, with good features for hands and feet.

### ⑤ Kaiser      39m HVS 5a
*FA Richard Corbett & Derrick Jones 1962*

A regal line sweeping through the best features of the buttress.

**1. 15m 5a** Start as for *Cima*, climb to a good thread belay in the recess.

**2. 24m 4c** Move rightwards around the rib, traverse into the corner, then across the right wall and up the arête to finish.

### ⑥ Power Trap      36m E3 5c
*FFA Pat Littlejohn & Steve Jones 1970*

Power up the smooth right wall of the gully towards the curving crack above. Follow the crack diagonally leftwards, keeping off the arête at the top.

### ⑦ South Pillar Rib      36m HS 4a
*FA Jeremy Talbot & Richard Corbett 1962*

A good route: follow the groove, pillar, wall and arête, taking care with the rock to finish. Can easily be split into two pitches.

### 6 The Jewel 15m VS 4c

*FA Andy Sharp & John Harwood 20th March 1982*

Follows a cheeky line up the shallow groove in the wall, stepping right to finish up the final corner.

### 7 Sharp Eyed 15m E5 6a

*FA Martin Crocker & Matt Ward 11th July 1987*

Follow pockets left to the break, then move right on better holds to a flake and sweep back left to finish.

### 8 Crypt 15m E2 5b

*FA John Bullock & Gwyn Evans 9th December 1984*

Often wet and always exciting. Head up the corner crack, then follow the steep ground leftwards to finish.

## RIGHT WALL

SS 4195 8718

**Aspect**: SW

### 9 Franceschi 15m E2 5b

*FFA Andy Sharp & John Harwood 20th March 1982*

A bold route with an energetic crux. Start below the middle of the overhang, climbing directly to it past a small thread at the back of the roof. Pull strenuously around the roof, finishing rightwards up the groove. A direct finish can be made at 5c through steeper ground.

### 10 Treason 15m E4 6b

*FA Andy Sharp 5th November 1987*

A hard route up the middle of the wall. Start below where the overhang becomes just an overlap and climb direct to an old rusty peg. A long reach to unfriendly holds leads to the finishing groove.

### 11 Gamma 11m VS 4c

*FA Richard Corbett & P. Perkins 1962*

Follow the steep groove, making use of the left wall at half height.

### 12 Beta 11m HS 4b

*FA Richard Corbett & P. Perkins 1962*

A good line on solid rock, following the crack.

### 13 Midel 11m VD

*FA Richard Corbett & P. Perkins 1962*

The pleasing pillar of rock between the two cracks.

### 14 Alpha 7m D

*FA Jeremy Talbot & Richard Corbett 1962*

The short and easy seaward crack.

Mike Griffiths on *The Jewel* (VS 4c).
Photo: Matt Woodfield.

# THURBA HEAD

Some fine rock is hidden round the corner from the more frequented crags to the west, containing some good, serious and hard routes. This crag offers a real sense of adventure, it is rarely visited and so it should just be you, the rock and the sea... the constant sea.

The routes on the left need a low spring tide to gain the platform at their base. Other routes can either be started from the floor at very low water, or via a poorly protected traverse above the high water line. Can you swim with your rack on?

From the rocky ledge mentioned in the approach, descend the easy rib then traverse across the wall to gain the start of the following routes.

SS 4212 8689

**Aspect**: S

**Access agreements**: There is currently a restriction due to nesting birds on these routes from 1st March to 15th August. No climbing is allowed on Thurba Head during this period. This restriction is reviewed in May and lifted if nesting is completed early. For more information and updates see the BMC's Regional Access Database.

**1 The Thurba Pillar**     **36m E5 6b**

*FA Martin Crocker 7th September 1985*

An awesome route that takes a line up the eye-catching front pillar of the headland. From the base of the pillar, climb to gain the crack, stepping left into the recess at its end. Climb the slim pillar above on its right arête until better holds appear on the left. Make use of hairline cracks above and move through the angular groove to belay. Exit by scrambling off to the right.

**2 Earthly Powers**     **33m E5 6a**

*FA Pat Littlejohn & Tony Penning 14th June 1983*

Start below the obvious black groove line of the pillar.

**1. 15m 5b** Follow good holds to a cramped belay at the base of the groove.

Mewslade Bay, looking towards Thurba Head. Photo Stuart Llewellyn.

**2. 18m 6a** Traverse out right to gain the arête, moving back left underneath the overhangs. Continue up steep ground until the rock eases and belay. Scramble off right to finish.

### ③ Unearthly Power                     35m E5 6c
*FA Martin Crocker & John Harwood 7th February 1999*

**1. 15m 5b** As for *Earthly Powers*.
**2. 20m 6c** Bridge up the corner (small wires, no holds), moving right to finish up the steep head wall. Exit by scrambling off to the right.

### ④ Thin Ice                           24m E4 6a
*FA Martin Crocker & Gordon Jenkin 7th September 1985*

From the good ledge in the chimney of *Barnacle Bill*, traverse left then move over a bulge to gain the thin cracks and command the steep wall above.

### ⑤ Barnacle Bill                      24m E1 5b
*FFA John Bullock & Chris Lownds 28th July 1982*

Belay either in or below the difficult barnacle-filled chimney. Escape this to gain the crack and groove above.

### ⑥ Summer Wine                        24m E3 6a
*FA Pat Littlejohn & Tony Penning 14th June 1983*

A tough route with a desperate move onto the sloping ledge. Climb up to the overhang, passing it on its left to gain the crack above. Follow this with interest to the top.

### ⑦ Junior Jaws                        21m E1 5b
*FA Tony Penning & Dave Hope 5th September 1982*

Climb the shallow groove until it is possible to pull left around the arête and gain the obvious corner to finish.

### ⑧ Laughing Gear                      18m E1 5a
*FA Tony Penning & John Harwood 1982*

Take the shallow groove, with little in the way of protection.

### ⑨ Wimp                                   18m S
*FA Guy Richardson & Mike Danford 1982*

The easiest route here; head steeply up the groove on this short outing.

Mateusz Andrzejewski on the excellent *The Enema Affair* (F6a). Third Sister. Photo: Dan Carroll.

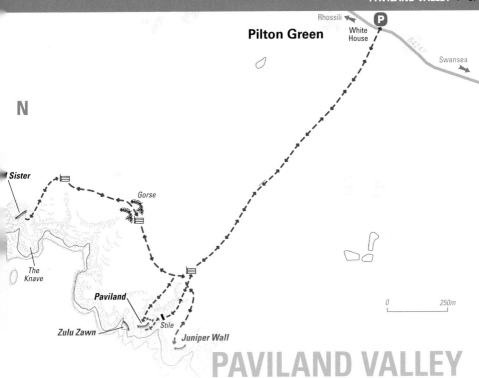

# PAVILAND VALLEY

This chapter contains a mixed array of venues and climbs in some of the peninsula's wildest and most rugged landscape. The longer-than-usual approaches means the rock friction is the best to be found; expect those little cuts around the fingernails (but so worth it).

The mega-classic trad crags of Paviland and Juniper Wall give big single-pitch cragging. Juniper Wall gives particularly good value for money for the VS and HVS climber. Paviland has first-rate climbing if sometimes a little esoteric, hidden between some fine botanical specimens. The atmospheric hard sport-wall of Zulu Zawn is tucked away in a brooding void below Paviland. A little stomp away is the tall, exposed buttress of the Third Sister, home to a first-rate collection of mid- to high-grade sport climbs.

The only venue which is tidal is Zulu Zawn, which can be accessed 3 hours either side of lower tide. Third Sister can be very cold when windy, but the sub F7a climbs don't seep allowing t-shirt-off climbing even in winter when there is little wind. Both Paviland and Juniper Wall can be absolute suntraps.

**Approach**: From Scurlage, take the B4247 signposted Rhossili and Pitton Cross Campsite. After a sharp right corner, look out for a lone white house on your left. Immediately opposite this house is an open area known as Pilton Green Farm; park here off the track on the grass. Cross the road and go through the wooden gate left of the house into the start of a series of fields. Keep to the right edge of these fields, through numerous gates and over bridges. As the coastline becomes clearer, an obvious valley dropping to the sea can be seen in front of you. Go through the wooden gate and then choose from the following.

The Knave and Third Sister looking out to Worms Head.
Photo: Wayne Tucker.

**Third Sister:** Turn right through the green gate and follow the worn path. Stick to the right-hand boundary for 300m to reach a gate. The path continues through high gorse bushes and, after a further 350m, reaches another gate. Continue up past the first valley and head down a second valley towards the coast before you reach the long stone wall. At the bottom of this is a 'fin of land' (the Knave) on the left-hand side, and the Third Sister is on your right.

**Paviland:** It's simplest to abseil in for Paviland, leaving your sacks at the top of the crag. It is also possible to walk in via an exposed scramble traverse.

Abseil approach: Turn right through the green gate and up the worn path. At the top of the hill is a coastal path signpost, from here head straight for the coastline. A notch on the left side of the cliff top contains an abseil ring (down and right when looking out to sea) that can and should be backed up with gear in the surrounding rock for your abseil.

Scramble approach: The scramble is very exposed and requires care. Walk down the valley following the stone wall and cross a stile at its end. Follow a dirt and scree path uphill and around, dropping down onto an isle of rock (possible gearing-up spot). Scramble up and traverse leftwards on big holds to a ledge system about 5m up. Follow ledges around the corner bringing you to the entrance of the famous Paviland cave.

**Zulu Zawn:** As for Paviland, either scramble or abseil in. From the base of Paviland crag, head right (when looking out to sea) across rocky terrain, until a scramble descent can be made down into the zawn.

**Juniper Wall:** Turn left and at the top of the hill head right towards the sea; the crag lies at the end of the promontory. The base can be reached by scrambling either left down a grassy slope or right down a small gully (when looking out to sea).

# THIRD SISTER

The Third Sister is an impending crag which has seen resurgence since some of the lines were turned into clip-ups. Steep rock, sharp holds, stunning views, no queues and a grade range of 5+ through to 7b+. What more could you ask for? It dries fast and rarely seeps, but is a hellish place to be when windy.

SS 4320 8634

**Aspect**: S

**1 Chilean Flame Thrower**      **12m F7b**

*FA Goi Ashmore 23rd April 2010*

Hard pulls through the leaning wall at the far end of the crag.

**2 World in Action**      **12m F7b+**

*FA Andy Sharp 1989*

Fingery technical climbing with a powerful start.

**3 Popped In, Souled Out**      **12m F7b**

*FA Andy Sharp & Pete Lewis 6th February 1988*

Another powerful start leading to a technical midsection, followed by thuggy climbing to its end.

**4 French Undressing**      **12m F6c+**

*FA Andy Sharp & Pete Lewis 10th August 1988*

Begins to the right of the 'pterodactyl' cave at half height. Make a powerful sequence through the lip, which is followed by easier moves to the lower off.

**5 Twilight World**      **12m F6c**

*FA Andy Sharp & Pete Lewis 10th October 1987*

A superb route on excellent holds up the vague arête. (Probably the best route at the crag.)

**6 Southeast Wall**      **13m F6a+**

*FA Andy Sharp & Pete Lewis 1986*

A good climb taking the apparent scoop and groove. The majority of the holds are very sharp and sometimes painful.

**7 Fiesta**      **14m F6a+**

*FA Andy Sharp & Pete Lewis 10th October 1987*

Enjoyable moves on good rock following a crack and groove. Joins *Southeast Wall* at the top to share the same lower off.

**8 Sister Mary's Blessed Finger**      **22m F5+**

*FA Roy Thomas 9th August 2009*

A pleasant outing on steep terrain; the route may feel harder than the grade for those not used to this angle. Head up the ramp and overcome the bulge. A long runout on an easy scramble takes you to the main steep wall; climb this on good holds.

**9 The Enema Affair**      **22m F6a**

*FA Roy Thomas 9th August 2009*

Shares a start and lower-off with *Sister Mary's Blessed Finger*. From the ledge, take the right-hand variant starting with good flake holds. Progress can be a little blind but the holds are there.

Chris Shepherd attempting to negotiate with *Ultimatum* (F7c).
Photo: Make The Next Move Images.

# ZULU ZAWN

This striking steep wall hidden beneath Paviland crag has two hard sport routes in residence. The wall suffers from seepage, so will need a prolonged dry spell and low tides for best conditions. Access is available 2 hours either side of low water.

SS 4367 8587

**Aspect**: SW

## ① Zulu Wall 20m F8a

*FA Adrian Berry 2010*

Climb the striking natural line of the wall with increased steepness on moderate jugs. A string of moves through a hard bouldery section either takes you to the lower off or catching some air.

## ② Ultimatum 19m F7c

*FA Simon Rawlinson 3rd June 2010*

The line of weakness on the right of the wall. A tricky sequence leads you up the wall until a big flake is reached. From here, launch rightwards with a beautiful drop knee or a wild slap to a ramp line that leads to the lower off.

## THE RED LADY OF PAVILAND

A major discovery took place in the Paviland Cave (see next page) in 1823 when Reverend William Buckland abseiled down and entered the cave, hoping to find reported elephant tusks and bones. Along with these, he unearthed a complete human skeleton on the left-hand side of the cave. Since the bones were dyed red in colour, Buckland wrongly assumed he had found a lady of the night from Roman times who was buried far away from civilised society. After Buckland's death, the remains were re-examined and the 'Red Lady of Paviland' was actually found to be a man who lived in significantly older times than the initial assessment. Carbon dating revealed that the remains belonged to a man in his 20s who was buried 33,000 years ago, making these the oldest human remains discovered in the UK. Although now on the coast, the cave was originally 70 miles inland overlooking a plain. One modern theory of the fate of the 'Red Lady' is that he lost his life while hunting a mammoth. The rest of the hunting party laid his remains to rest in the shelter of the cave along with the skull of the mammoth that killed their companion as a ceremonial tribute.

Charles Romijn.

# PAVILAND

This adventurous crag is less vegetated than it first seems (honestly!) and the routes described are very much worth a visit with some quality rock between the plant pots. The rock is mostly sound with a multitude of natural threads, some of which are in situ. Make sure you take plenty of slings and have your prusik cords handy for the small ones. JRR Tolkien fans will see a running theme with some of the route names.

Paviland Cave, the 'Cradle of Wales', is located at the base of the crag to the right. The crag has a large exposed groove on its right side which splits its grassy base (*Liang Shan Po* starts to the left of this). Many of the climbs share a pedestal at two-thirds height in a niche known as The Ring stance.

Descent can be made by walking inland and using the grassy slope back down onto the path leading to the isle of rock to repeat the exposed traverse.

SS 4368 8586

**Aspect**: S

 **Liang Shan Po**                    **45m E1 5b**

*FA Jeremy Talbot & Chris Connick 1977*

To access the start of this route, scramble down and to the other side of the exposed gully. Climb up the slab then, using an indistinct crack, pass through a small overhang halfway up. From here head direct and then through the overhang past a peg; finish direct.

② **The Ring**                                **38m HS 4b**

*FA Jeremy Talbot & Chris Connick 1976*

A peninsula classic taking the HS leader though some wild terrain for the grade. From the bottom of the groove, climb leftwards to an obvious hole across a calcite featured slab. Head straight up to the niche above (possible belay) then test your might up the final crack past good threads, finishing rightwards.

③ **Babylon**                                **38m HVS 5a**

*FA Jeremy Talbot & Chris Connick 1977*

Takes a parallel line to the right of *The Ring*. Climb through a broken trough and then use cracks above to reach the pedestal. In the upper section take the first crackline in front of you, finishing to the left of *Half Dome*.

④ **Half Dome**                              **36m E2 5c**

*FA Andy Sharp & John Harwood 1st January 1985*

Climb the slab left of the groove to an old thread. Move rightwards initially then follow an arched path left to a possible belay on *The Ring* stance. Step right off the pedestal into the second crackline with an old thread, finishing straight up.

⑤ **East Gully Groove**                      **36m HVS 5a**

*FA Jeremy Talbot & Chris Connick 1976*

Follow the obvious central groove which splits the crag. The climbing doesn't really start until you reach the half-

📷 Matt Woodfield belaying Chris
Mathewson into the lair of *Shelob* (HS 4b)
before escaping through the exit hole.
Photo: Stuart Llewellyn.

height cave, but it is an excellent route with good gear and lots of in situ threads. Pop into the half-height cave and visit Jeremy Talbot's workshop if it takes your fancy.

### 6 Fellowship of the Ring      42m E1 5c

*FA Jeremy Talbot & Chris Connick 1977*

A traverse of the crag that starts from the small cave in *East Gully Groove*.

**1. 9m 5c** Follow a leftwards-rising traverse line, with some moments of difficulty, towards a small niche of *The Ring* stance.

**2. 12m 5a** Move and continue your traverse adventure left across a steep section and enter a deep groove; belay at the bottom of this groove.

**3. 21m 4c** Climb towards the overhang above before moves left gain a pedestal. Continue traversing left into the next groove. Climb this for a few metres, before stepping left below a small overhang and undercut wall. Finish up a final wide groove.

### 7 Shelob      36m HS 4b

*FA Jeremy Talbot & Chris Connick 1976*

Best done in two pitches for no other reason than to get a better view of the leader's struggles while exiting. Climb the vegetated slab via any line to the cave, possible belay. (Look out for big spiders, Frodo.) Watch in anticipation as your mate climbs the right wall, then traverses left to begin the struggle of wriggling through the exit hole. Laugh as they get stuck and realise the horrible slab was worth it ... just!

# JUNIPER WALL

This is a brilliant venue with excellent rock friction and superb routes. The crag hides an abundance of both holds and gear in a sheltered sun trap. Don't be fooled by its slabby look, once on route you'll soon find your arms getting a work out.

There are two girdles following obvious lines across the crag; these are referred to in some route descriptions. Several routes share 'The Junction' stance on the high slab, the pegs are rotten but other gear is available.

SS 4381 8581

**Aspect**: S

**1 Killer's Route** 42m E2 5b

*FA Gwyn Evans & John Bullock June 1982*

**1. 20m 4c** Head up to the triangular niche, pull through its overlap and head to the helay of The Junction.

**2. 22m 5b** Traverse right for 3m before pulling up and onto an overhung ledge. Continue rightwards through another corner, finishing rightwards.

**2 The Jackal Finish** 19m E2 5c

*FA John Bullock & Gwyn Evans June 1982*

Get to The Junction via any route, then stare in wonderment at the ancient bolts and pegs that are long past their use-by date. Climb into the corner above before swinging left onto a rib. Make moves left past the rib and pull up right. From here either branch off left and follow the groove line, or make moves to a ledge and finish up steep ground.

**3 Assassin** 44m HVS 5a

*FA John Bullock & Roy Thomas 22nd June 1980*

Arguably the best HVS on Gower and the classic of the crag, following the rightward-slanting groove. Totter up the slab into the sustained crack that takes you to a shallow niche around 20m; twin cracks are used above this. Move right at the bulge, then back left into and up a broken groove. A benchmark at the grade.

**4 Barracuda** 44m E5 6a

*FA Andy Sharp & John Harwood 3rd July 1982*

A bold climb with lengthy runouts.

**1. 20m 6a** Climb the initial slabs, placing a good high nut in the diagonal crack of *Hair Raiser* for protection before beginning up the protruding wall on crozzly flakes. A long runout follows, with hard sustained climbing to a jam crack. Place gear shortly after, then easier ground yields to The Junction.

**2. 22m 5b** Finish up the second pitch of *Killer's Route*.

**5 Perch** 39m E1 5b

*FA Gwyn Evans & John Bullock 8th October 1989*

Head off below the rather large jammed block. Manoeuvre onto this from the left and take a direct path up the wall above using thin cracks to the break of *Dry Riser*. Climb the wall above, keeping a few metres right of *Assassin*'s groove to finish.

**6 Hitman** 36m HVS 4c

*FA Swansea University Mountaineering Club 1968*

This shares a start with *Perch*. From the jammed block step right and take a rightward-sloping crack towards the break of *Dry Riser*. Cross diagonally right over a sheet of rock into an awkward groove (*Task Force*). Climb the groove leftwards to the top.

**7 Task Force** 35m VS 4c

*FA Mike Harber & Clive Horsfield 1982*

Begin at a small recess below a rightwards-slanting groove. Continue using this groove and crack heading towards the break of *Dry Riser*. From this point tackle the awkward groove above and left. Finish over broken ground.

**8 Ninja** 34m VS 4b

*FA Chris Allen & Mike Danford 1990*

Step up to the protruding block before following a zig zag crack towards a small niche immediately below *Dry Riser*. Go through black-streaked rock to a triangular niche, and finish rightwards across broken rock.

**9 On the Horizon** 33m VS 4b

*FA Guy Richardson & J. Pratt 1981*

Follow the parallel cracks rightwards towards the horizon. From the recess finish direct over unstable rock.

### 10 Hair Raiser — 56m HVS 5a

*FA Mike Harber & S. Robinson 1982*

A stunning first pitch, unfortunately let down by the second which is a merely a means of escaping the crag. The first pitch is worth it, however.

**1. 36m 5a** Wander across the lower rising traverse line before fighting the steepening bulging shield of rock using big hand holds between the plants. Continue to a small recess after the break has petered out and belay here.

**2. 20m 4b** Head left to the overlap, then down climb onto a black section before pulling over the overlap and cautiously making ground left to belay in the descent gully.

### 11 Socialist Worker — 39m VS 4b

*FA Len Moran & K. Snook 1977*

From the black-stained triangle, follow cracks leftwards towards *Dry Riser*. Traverse further left to the awkward groove (*Task Force*), climbing this to finish over broken terrain.

### 12 Dry Riser — 67m HVS 4c

*FA Mike Harber & John Mothersele 1977*

The fantastic climbing on pitch one contrasts with the blind and insecure second pitch.

**1. 36m 4c** Climb the upper rising traverse line from the far right of the crag, then make for The Junction and belay.

**2. 20m 4c** Traverse left towards a small corner and blindly struggle through the overlap. Continue across the vegetated slab, belaying in the descent gully.

Dan Carroll at The Junction before venturing onto *The Jackal Finish* (E2 5c). Photo: Stuart Llewellyn.

Jacky Tyrie leading the excellent *Direct* (VS 4c) at Boiler Slab. Photo: Stuart Llewellyn.

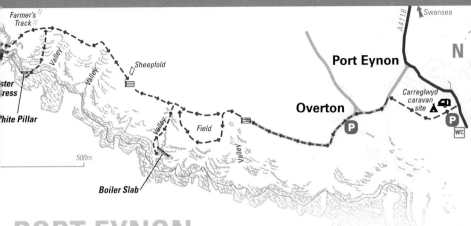

# PORT EYNON

Port Eynon is a well-frequented tourist spot in the middle of the peninsula with an easily accessible beach, a handful of shops and several caravan parks. The climbing in this area is best accessed via Overton, just before entering Port Eynon. Fantastic walking is available along this fabulous stretch of coastline.

Boiler Slab is the jewel in the area, and is a great day out if you're part of a group in need of a good range of grades. White Pillar and Easter Buttress provide more tranquil alternatives, each with their own unique charm.

**Approach**: Just before Port Eynon is a right-hand turn for Overton village. There is limited parking available so please park considerately. Should you need to look elsewhere for parking, turn around and drive to Port Eynon where there is a large pay-and-display car park; this simply adds a pleasant 10 minute walk. From Port Eynon's car park, enter the Carreglwyd caravan site and fork left past the barrier until you reach a stile on the far side. A path then leads through two fields and onto Overton road. Turn left and follow the road past the triangular green.

From Overton, walk to the end of the road and follow a farm track rightwards at the gate. At the end of this track cross another gate with stone supports, and continue along the footpath past a valley. At the top of the slope follow the path around or cut through the big field,

leading you to the top of another valley. From here select your crag.

**Boiler Slab:** Follow the valley towards the coast; the crag appears on your left.

**White Pillar:** A bit tricky to find on your first visit. Keep following the coastal path, passing through a gate after 300m. Continue past the first dry valley and drop down the second, easiest on the path on its far side. Continue down the slope and bend off right, scrambling down to the base of the crag which sits on the bottom of the headland.

**Easter Buttress:** As for White Pillar to the top of the second dry valley, then continue for another 100m where you'll need your eagle eyes open to spot a farm track that appears on the right. From here head seawards and slightly right until you can descend down the left side of a ridge. Pass underneath a buttress and cross over the ridge, scramble all the way down and round left to the base of the crag. For the start of most routes you must make the big step across the zawn to gain ledges on the other side.

# EASTER BUTTRESS

A recent addition to Gower, this sea-level crag has been overlooked for years and offers a range of pleasant lower-grade routes. The rock is split into three sections: the bottom is solid, the mid-section easy ledges on sharp rock and the finishes are terrifyingly loose and should be treated with care. The base of the crag is washed by the sea allowing access about 3 hours either side of low water, although it is possible to abseil down to ledges above the sea at any time.

SS 4404 8570

**Aspect**: S

### 1 Midwife Crisis      35m VS 5a

*FA Nick Smith & Peter Morgan 15th September 2009*

A quirky route offering variety and interest. Start in the cave on the left at the base of the crag.

**1. 15m 4a** At the back of the cave climb up onto the shelf of rock and move right, exiting through the hole above. Follow easily up ledges to the base of the upper cave.

**2. 20m 5a** Climb steeply up the wall on the left side of the cave on pockets. Cross to the apex of the cave and finish up the easy gully, taking care with the rock.

### 2 Empty Cave      35m HS 4a

*FA John Roberts & Nick Smith 7th April 2009*

Start on a fin of rock just over the bad step, below the black overhanging nose. Climb up the wall and round to the left of the root. Continue up the wall on the right side of the cave, which leads to cracks up the final headwall.

### 3 Cream Egg      35m HS 4a

*FA Nick Smith & John Roberts 7th April 2009*

Start to the right of the black overhanging nose of rock; climb up the slab to gain the obvious corner crack. Continue up through the easy middle section then move right and ascend the head wall, stepping left into a groove to finish.

### 4 April Fools      35m S

*FA John Roberts & Nick Smith 7th April 2009*

Climb the right wall of the corner to gain the groove above that leads to the easy ledges. Finish with care up the final loose corner.

### 5 Chocolate Bunny      35m VD

*FA Nick Smith & John Roberts 7th April 2009*

Climb the obvious corner groove bounding the right side of the face, taking care with the rock to finish.

### 6 Easter Parade      35m VD

*FA Nick Smith & John Roberts 7th April 2009*

Climb pleasantly to and along the obvious curving line on the right wall of the crag, starting where the sea allows.

# WHITE PILLAR

White Pillar is a pleasant almost non-tidal venue that offers a refreshing break from the crowds often found at the more popular Boiler Slab. The rock is quick to dry, but this can be a windy spot. Although the base of the crag is tidal, available about 4 hours either side of low water, all routes can be started higher up on the approach ledges.

**WARNING**

When you lift a jigsaw in the air from one end it magically stays complete, but poke it and it starts to fall into pieces. The right side of the top of this crag is like this, and care should be taken not to 'poke' too hard.

SS 4412 8558
**Aspect**: S

**1  Crack and Slab**                                      **25m VD**

*FA Jeremy Talbot 1967*

Climb up cracks on the left side of the pillar, moving right to finish up the groove in the wall.

**2  West Kante**                                           **25m S 4a**

*FA Jeremy Talbot 1967*

A fine line taking you up the centre of the pillar, starting directly below the century box. Climb to and through the century box, leaving it via cracks on the left that lead up to a ledge. Continue up the face past a slab to finish up the final headwall.

**3  Grey Slab**                                            **27m S**

*FA Jeremy Talbot 1967*

Climb up to the left side of the lowest overhang, traversing rightwards underneath this to its end. From here follow the groove above, moving left where it peters out and respecting the fragile nature of the rock.

**4  Sizzler**                                              **47m E1 5a**

*FA John Harwood 16th August 1987*

A bold route with good but spaced protection. Start on the end of the descent ledge below the overhangs. Follow cracks up to the lower band, moving through this and the other two. Move leftwards over the easy ground and finish up the final technical wall.

**5  Bermuda Shorts**                                       **20m HS 4a**

*FA John Harwood 16th August 1987*

A climb that starts well but resembles a Jenga tower in its upper reaches. Take a line up the right side of the pillar, starting directly under the right side of the second overhang. Climb up and into the groove following this to the top, taking extra care with the rock.

# BOILER SLAB

This venue gets its name from the boiler of an old shipwreck which used to rest on the sea below. It is an excellent summer venue, combining climbing and rock pool exploration.

The crag itself is a large slab with a roof towards its right end. It faces southwest, getting the sun from late morning onwards. Strong winds can blast onto the slab, most noticeably on the right-hand routes; this does mean it dries relatively quickly after a shower. The slab is non-tidal and, in the most part, a gentle inviting angle. It is a well-frequented area as the amount of polishing on the easier routes demonstrates, but they are still excellent outings as the rock is generally very good quality. A scramble over some broken terrain at the base of the crag is needed to get to the start of the climbs. Descent is a walk-off via the obvious path down a slope at the back of the face.

SS 4505 8501

**Aspect**: SW

**1 Classic**     **19m HD**

FA Alan Osborne & Brian Taylor 1949

A fine line, which takes the corner on the left of the main slab. This popular route is one of Gower's earliest climbs.

**2 Column**     **19m S 4a**

FA Jeremy Talbot 1967

Head up the wall between a groove on your left and a pillar on your right. Get to a depression in the rock, surmount this and use ledges to the top.

**3 Dulfer**     **19m S 4a**

FA Alan Osborne & Brian Taylor 1949

An absorbing climb following the obvious corner feature, bearing right until it peters out. Swoop round left at the break and climb into the groove, using ledges to finish.

**4 Swirtler**     **21m HVS 5b**

FA T. Moon & C. Maybury 1973

A fine route with the difficulty at the start (the first few moves are hard to protect). Start on a smooth slab, just left of a bulging corner then head straight up the wall.

**5 Direct**     **21m VS 4c**

FA Jeremy Talbot 1968

A popular outing, mixing thuggery with subtlety. Begin at a rib on a slab with black streaks. Climb this rib, moving left to overcome the arch using a good flake. Continue up the slab to the second of two small roofs, passing it on the left and climbing direct through the bulges to finish.

**6 Termination**     **21m HVS 5a**

FA Peter Hinder & V. Rees 1970

An engaging line with fiddly gear placements. Start underneath a patch of ivy, head to it and then use a thin crack above until it fades out. Escape left under the roof and exit on bulges.

**7 Nuclear Arms**     **22m E2 5c**

FA Andy Sharp & John Harwood 20th October 1985

A one-move wonder, but an excellent one! Get to the roof using *Termination*, load the back of the roof with gear, clip the wobbly peg runner and go. Nice entry E2.

### 8 Middle Age Dread                     22m E3 6a

*FA Andy Sharp & John Harwood 20th October 1985*

A daring route at the top end of the grade for exposure. Begin at a rightward facing groove, then climb boldly through the overlap and head up the slab under the looming roof. Use the peg runner on *Nuclear Arms*, then take the roof on at its widest point. Make use of a thin undercut in the roof and a small flake above. Tough for the grade.

### 9 Nemo                     18m VS 4c

*FA Peter Hinder 1970*

Start at the left edge of the recess, and climb to a cracked groove. Make a move right and head up towards an upper groove. Go through this and the overhangs above, before surmounting the protruding block directly. Take care.

### 10 Tokyo                     21m E1 5c

*FA Andy Sharp & John Harwood 20th October 1985*

You're going over the widest part of the overlap. Get gear underneath and use technique or a long reach from a good jug to a good distant flake. With the hard bit over, be rewarded with the smell of lemon and dance up the slab to finish through the bulges.

### 11 Tokyo II                     21m HVS 5b

*FA Gwyn Evans & K. Snook 1988*

A route on which to practise your faith in friction and rockovers. Start 2m right of the older brother at a thin crack, climbing over the overlap and up the slab. Continue straight up to finish.

### 12 Ayesha                     21m VS 4c

*FA Jeremy Talbot 1971*

A tense excellent climb beginning at the right side of the overlap. Head up the slab using a series of undercut flakes. Finish up the arête, to the left of the obvious broken groove of *Pinnacle Crack*. For extra exposure, pick a windy day.

### 13 Pinnacle Crack                     21m VD

*FA Jeremy Talbot 1969*

Easy and pleasant. Take the obvious broken groove and finish between an arête and a pinnacle of rock. Take care on the upper section; some parts are a little loose.

### 14 Overhang Traverse                     28m VS 4c

*FA C. Maybury & T. Moon 28th December 1977*

Set off up *Dulfer* and continue until you are level with a small roof. Make moves rightwards to this before traversing further under the main roof. Exit on the right side of the roof through the groove.

### 15 Girdle                     38m VS 4c

*FA Gwyn Evans & Guy Richardson 28th December 1977*

Begin up *Classic* and traverse the horizontal crack which splits the crag at half height. Follow this rightwards to the end of the crag. Finish up either for *Ayesha* or *Pinnacle Crack*.

Kat Torr tottering up *Dulfer* (S 4a) with Jacky Tyrie belaying. Photo: Stuart Llewellyn.

Gareth Tucker on *Bitchin'*
(F7b+), Red Sea Walls.
Photo: Oli Buxton.

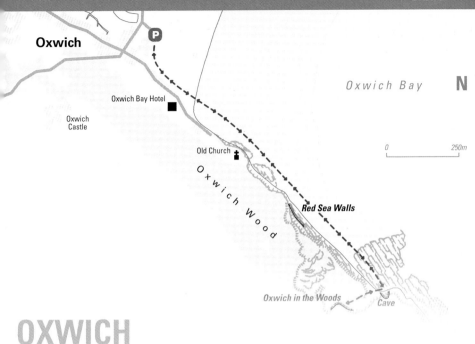

Oxwich

Oxwich Bay Hotel

Oxwich Castle

Old Church

Oxwich Wood

Oxwich Bay

N

0   250m

Red Sea Walls

Oxwich in the Woods   Cave

# OXWICH

Oxwich bay is an expanse of stunning flat golden sands; it is very popular during the summer season with anyone who enjoys a great day out by the sea. The bay takes in some of the best scenery the Gower has to offer: directly across the bay lie the Tors and Three Cliffs and if you follow the coastline further south towards the tip you'll see Pennard.

The faces reach up to 15m in places and, in the case of Red Sea Walls, they range from just off vertical to severely overhanging. The angle at Oxwich in the Woods is a little more welcoming but only just; as a result it contains an easier spectrum of climbs. Access to the crags is tidal, which can be gained 2 hours 30 mins either side of low tide.

The area has a number of very worthwhile climbs which really pack a punch. Avoid climbing here during high humidity or after heavy rain as the faces are likely to be very wet. The very shady Oxwich in the Woods can offer good shelter from small showers due to its protected position among the trees, although the crag needs a couple of days to dry out after a soaking. Red Sea Walls

receives early morning sun and will be in the shade by midday. Routes here are affected by seepage after rain.

**Approach:** The turnoff for Oxwich is adjacent to the remains of a small castle gatehouse, signposted 'Oxwich Bay Hotel'. Follow a narrow road down a steep hill and along a flat stretch for approximately 1 mile. Parking is available on the left, where a fee is payable at the gate. Alternatively, the Oxwich Bay Hotel provides parking for its customers, taking a signposted left turn passing the shop on your right.

**Red Sea Walls:** From either car park head out onto the sand, and begin to follow the right edge of the beach until the cliff is in view after 5 minutes.

**Oxwich in the Woods:** Continue along rocky terrain

Path into woodland

for a few more minutes until a wide but squat cave can be seen. A well-hidden path leads up a slope into a woodland area right of the cave, taking you to the quarried walls.

**Access agreements:** Oxwich Bay is special coastline for the study of classic coastal forms and habitats between dunes, beach and cliffs. Being a Site of Special Scientific Interest (SSSI), climbers should use the approaches described, avoid all vegetation damage and use the bolt lower offs installed below the cliff top. The general public are not encouraged to use the woodland areas.

## RED SEA WALLS

The Red Sea Walls were a major sport climbing find back in the late 1990s, giving us mega-classics such as *Kissin' the Pink* (F6c) and *Bitchin'* (F7b+). A large section of the crag has fallen down after a winter storm a few years ago, leaving some of Gower's hardest sport routes now a little closer to the sea (a handful of which never saw a second ascent). The routes are steep and a tenacious approach is required as, in many cases, the cruxes are right at the end. SS 5064 8589

**Aspect**: NE

Oxwich Towers.
Photo: Rob Howell.

### 1 Beyond All Resin                    14m F6b+
*FA Roy Thomas & Gary Gibson 28th May 1995*

A crackline in the woods on an arête. A feisty start on pockets under the arête, finishing in the jam crack.

### 2 Resin d'etre                        14m F7a+
*FA Roy Thomas 1995*

Can be located by the circular hole at 3m. A technical line with fingery moves to the bitter end.

### 3 Two of a Perfect Pair               14m F7b+
*FA Eugene Travers-Jones 29th July 1996*

Climb the shallow groove and wall, with a hard-to-miss glued-on hold and massive staple. Difficulties come at the start with the glued-on hold. Easily move up the groove before a hard undercut yields to bigger holds and the lower off.

### 4 Red River Rock                      14m F7b
*FA Gary Gibson 16th August 1997*

Super fingery wall climbing on edges and crimps up the bubbly wall, breaking left at the fourth bolt to use the flake and then the lower off of *Two of a Perfect Pair*.

### 5 The Milkier Way                     14m F7c
*FA Gary Gibson 26th August 1997*

Follows the white streak and can be chalky. Thin crimps are in abundance although the climbing is steep, desperate and sustained throughout.

### 6 Mars Attacks                        13m F7a+
*FA Gary Gibson 19th July 1997*

Very good face climbing, taking the shallow groove and finishing via a slight arête.

### 7 Red with Rage                       16m F7a+
*FA Gary Gibson & Roy Thomas 1st July 1995*

Takes on the obvious sloping feature at two-thirds height; cool conditions could be advantageous. Excellent sustained climbing on good flakes all the way to its finale. At the top end of the grade.

### 8 Red Letter Day                      13m F7b+
*FA Gary Gibson 19th July 1999*

A good direct line with a difficult move right at its end; pumpy crimpy climbing throughout.

**⑨ Written in Red**         **14m F7b**

*FA Gary Gibson 6th July 1997*

Shares the first half of *Red Letter Day*, then slopes off right to a large flake from where you take a diagonal path to a separate lower off.

**⑩ Red Snapper**         **14m F7b+**

*FA Gary Gibson 19th July 1999*

Climbs through the undercut section of wall, utilising small crimps and pockets via an initial powerful move. The line then trends leftwards at the top. Never desperate, but the moves keep coming.

**⑪ Bitchin'**         **13m F7b+**

*FA Gary Gibson 26th August 1997*

A classic of the crag and one for the technicians. Sharp sustained crimpy climbing with an easy-to-mess-up finish.

**⑫ The Morgue the Merrier**     **13m F7b+**

*FA Gary Gibson 2nd July 1997*

A steady start leads to a bouldery sequence, where a heel hook may unlock the upper scooped wall to the lower off.

**⑬ Missin' the Drink**         **15m F7a+**

*FA Gary Gibson 2nd August 1997*

Described as both "rubbish" and "mean". A short, hard wall leads to a ledge, then long moves up dirty rock gain the finish groove of *Kissin' the Pink*, sharing its lower off.

**⑭ Kissin' the Pink**         **17m F6c**

*FA Eugene Travers-Jones, Gary Gibson & Roy Thomas 9th October 1994*

A superb route, certainly one of the best sport routes on the peninsula. Yard and power scream, or use technique and style to send this steep stunner. A tough sequence on the lower band leads to better holds on tufa pipes, pockets and other flowstone fun higher up, before the top groove offers respite and the finale. An alternative harder finish mantels the bulge on the right to gain the lower off (6c+).

**⑮ Milkin' the Link**         **15m F6b**

*FA Stuart Llewellyn & Steve Warrington 25th March 2012*

A filler in, but a great warm up for the steep affairs. Climb the tough start of *Kissin' the Pink* to the ledge, and follow the flake ramp rightwards, using a runner bolt of *Pissin' the Sink* to its very own lower off. Easiest for a second to get the quickdraws back.

**16 Pissin' the Sink**      **15m F7b+**

*FA Gary Gibson 20th July 1997*

Start left of the big thread and climb the steep wall directly to a desperate sloping finish. Can feel a little run out.

**17 Foaming at the Gusset**      **14m F7a+**

*FA Roy Thomas 1st July 1997*

Gain the ledge at one-third height. Use a large side pull to make direct progress, before following small stepped corners difficultly to the end.

**18 Inspector Glueseau**      **14m F6c+**

*FA Roy Thomas 1st July 1995*

A good and popular route. Climb up and onto the ledge, where a perplexing ramp trends rightwards. At the top of this make hard pulls left to reach the lower off.

**19 Glue Year**      **13m F7a**

*FA Roy Thomas 1995*

Climb to the right of a cheesy corner with a small triangular roof. Pull up through a red and white corner before a small roof leads to a tough finale.

**20 Settin' Stone**      **12m F7b+**

*FA Gary Gibson 25th August 1997*

An awkward low down move past the void, to get into a good horizontal crackline. Make progress up the smooth ramp to a good drilled rail beneath the roof. Pull left to a flake at the roof before moving onto the wall above.

**21 Steel Yourself**      **11m F6a+**

*FA Roy Thomas 1st July 1995*

The easiest climb here, with its difficulties at its climax. To climb at the suggested grade approach from the right off the undercut shelf. Climb a vague arête before difficult moves left lead to the lower off in a groove. A direct start may no longer be possible, as the starting boulder has relocated (6c+).

### OXWICH BOULDERING

During a winter storm in 2009 the Red Sea Walls crag suffered a major rockfall, sadly destroying many routes and devastating the surrounding woodland. Continued overleaf ...

Nik Goile *Kissin' the Pink* (F6c)
Photo Oli Bixton.

The upshot is that the house-sized chunks that remain have offered plentiful bouldering potential in addition to some original smaller blocks.

There is an array of size, shapes, features and grades to be solved. The sea and its inhabitants have begun to take their mark on the blocks (expect sore hands from the barnacles). The landings vary from soft and sandy to as many crash pads and spotters as can be accumulated. Collecting limpets and strategically placing them for foot and/or handholds is a dubious but imaginative tactic.

With a bit of exploration among the jumble, there are enough blocks for a session in its own right; alternatively, combine a spot of bouldering with the sport climbs and a day at the beach.

# OXWICH IN THE WOODS

Tucked away just off the shoreline is a forest that has a collection of sport climbs in surroundings that contrast markedly with Gower's usual golden sand and rock pool backdrops. The quarried walls here offer slightly easier-angled climbs with a good range of grades, but can be dirty. This is a Special Area of Conservation so please keep your impact to a minimum and use the main paths in front of the quarried faces. Being sheltered by the forest, climbing is possible during light rain showers. Many of the routes had their bolts replaced in 2011.
SS 5076 8562

**Aspect**: N

## LEFT-HAND SIDE

 **Load of Bullocks** 6m F6a+

*FA Roy Thomas 2005*

A route on its own on a short buttress to the left. Climb between good crimp edges.

📷 Battling the hurt locker on one of the house-sized blocks.
Photo: Jamie Maddison.

**2 Underneath the Larches**      13m F6b+

*FA Gary Gibson 2005*

The first route on the main wall proper. Use the left arête gaining it via a thin crack.

**3 Life's Too Short**      13m F6c

*FA Gary Gibson 2005*

Vertical wall climbing using some long reaches and edges to make a crucial clip. Runout around half height.

**4 Snatched from the Cradle**      13m F6b

*FA Gary Gibson 2005*

Avoids using the holds in the prominent groove, taking the wall on the left.

**5 Cradle Snatcher**      14m F6a

*FA Gary Gibson 2005*

Climbs the prominent groove. A little 'oomph' is needed to surmount the overlap.

**6 Baby Going Boing Boing**      14m F6b+

*FA Gary Gibson 2005*

Tackle the bulge low down and veer right, teetering up the shallow niche to a powerful ending and a shared lower off.

**7 Laughing Boy**      14m F7b+

*FA Gary Gibson 16th July 2005*

A pumpy climb, taking the centre of the leaning wall to finish over the square-cut ledge and the same lower off as *Baby Going Boing Boing*.

**8 Baby Bouncer**      14m F6c+

*FA Gary Gibson 17th July 2005*

A tough start leads into good face climbing through small overlaps.

**9 Teenage Kicks**      13m F6c+

*FA Gary Gibson 17th July 2005*

Takes the indistinct arête, with good moves to the top.

© Stuart Llewellyn on *My Inheritance (F6b)*.
Photo: Matt Woodfield.

### 10 My Inheritance       13m F6b

*FA Gary Gibson 17th July 2005*

A little contrived but a good climb, taking the same start as *Ox-Over Moon*. Break away from the broken groove making use of a 'chicken head', moving underneath the corner with interest.

### 11 Ox-Over Moon       12m F6a+

*FA Gary Gibson 17th July 2005*

A hard move getting off the floor to gain the good holds of the broken groove. Can feel airy as you progress higher; bear right to the lower off.

## RIGHT-HAND SIDE

### 12 Dynamo Kiev       12m F7b+

*FA Gary Gibson 17th July 2005*

Intensely bouldery and strenuous. Begin with a leap to fingery holds.

### 13 Grated Expectations       12m F7a

*FA Gary Gibson 17th July 2005*

Fingery face climbing sweeping leftwards and curving right to a shared lower off.

### 14 Un-named 1       11m 1 F6c

*FA T Dhallu 2004*

Begin direct before moving into the square-cut groove, following this left to a shared lower off with *Grated Expectations*.

### 15 Suppose I Try       11m F6a

*FA Roy Thomas 2004*

Similar start to *Un-named 1*, making progress through the prominent groove.

### 16 Anal Gesia       10m F6b

*FA Roy Thomas 2004*

Awkward moves through the intricate face yields to an overlap, before a recessed groove leads to the lower off.

### 17 Un-named 2                    10m F6a+
*FA Nic O'Neil 2004*

Good climbing up
the groove
system.

### 18 Toxicology                    10m F6c+
*FA Gary Gibson 16th July 2005*

Steep wall climbing.

### 19 Hubble, Rubble                 10m F6b
*FA Roy Thomas & Gary Gibson 16th July 2005*

Good moves through the wall and corner at its top.

### 20 Soil and Shuvel                10m F6a+
*FA Roy Thomas 2004*

Fine climbing on the wall behind the tree.

### 21 Anoek Clear Missile            10m F6b
*FA Goi Ashmore & Roy Thomas 10th November 2004*

Thinly climb the pillar and wall to a shared lower off with
*Soil and Shuvel.*

### 22 Dirt Box                       10m F6b+
*FA Roy Thomas & Gary Gibson 17th July 2005*

Start on a featured wall that doesn't seem to have
many holds, and weave rightwards following the easier
crackline. Likely to be dirty.

### 23 Filthy Snatch                  10m F6b
*FA Roy Thomas 12th July 2005*

A slightly puzzling line up the blank-looking wall,
climbing slightly left of the bolts.

### 24 Cauldron of Satyr              10m F6b
*FA Gary Gibson 16th July 2005*

Tackles the crackline and seam with good moves
throughout.

### 25 Devil's Brew                   10m F6a+
*FA Roy Thomas 16th July 2005*

The lower bulge gives the difficulty, giving way to easier
ground.

📷 Steph Duits stepping off golden sands
and onto *Left Edge* (D).
Photo: Stuart Llewellyn.

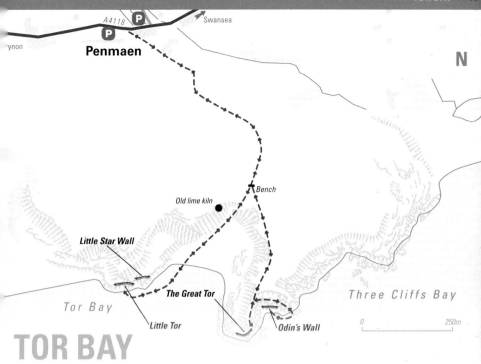

# TOR BAY

The climbs at neighbouring Three Cliffs Bay are the more famous and frequented but the climbing in Tor Bay is just as good, the scenery just as stunning and the crags quieter and less polished. The rock is generally steeper than at the other side of the bay, but the area still offers a range of grades (mostly at the lower end) and lengths from 7m to over 70m long. Don't forget your towel for an end-of-the-day swim.

**Approach**: From Parkmill, continue on the main road up the hill for about a mile to the village of Penmaen to a small car park (which is easily missed) just after the 30 limit signs. There's an overflow on the other side of the road for busy days. From the car park, go through the gate and down the track, heading right at the next gate. Continue along flat ground until you reach the wooden bench, from where the beach can be seen below.

**Little Tor** and **Little Star Wall:** Follow the path down to the beach and head rightwards across the sand towards the small headland; you can't miss it.

**Great Tor:** Walk out left along the path to where the headland becomes well defined, following the ridge then dropping down right to a saddle. A steep path leads you down left on grass then rock to the platform at the base of the ridge; the route itself is to your right as you descend. The seaward base of the tor can also be reached by walking around on sand at low tide across the beach from Little Tor, or around from Three Cliffs Bay to the east.

**Odin's Wall:** Approach as for the Great Tor until the start of the narrow headland. Here drop down to your left and follow steep grass and then rocky ledges that lead down to the beach.

# LITTLE TOR

Although overshadowed in size by its big brother to the east, Little Tor offers a fine selection of routes on quality rock. Climbing here has a real holiday feel being straight off the sand with low-graded routes and tourists looking on in admiration. The routes can be followed all the way to the top of the tor, but it's better to finish on the ledge and walk off as described.

**WARNING**

Belays at the top can be a bit hard to find; however, the rusty pegs should always be backed up!

Descent from the top is best made by walking off left (when facing the crag) along a ledge, then scrambling down ledges and along tracks back to the beach. The climbing is accessible about 4 hours either side of low water.

SS 5263 8777

**Aspect**: S

 **Left White**　　　　　**12m HVS 5a**

FA Chris Wyatt & Gwyn Evans May 2000

Technical climbing up the quartz slab with a bold finish.

 **Right Corner**　　　　　**17m S**

FA Jeremy Talbot & G. Jones 1959

Climb the obvious corner forming the start of the protruding pillar. Begin at the steep crack and climb this into the corner above.

**Left Edge (Tri Cornel)**　　　　　**18m D**

FA John Brailsford & St Athan MRT 1954

A surprisingly pleasant and engrossing climb, making use of cracks and ledges on the left edge of the pillar. Go up the blunt arête to the underhung corner then continue up grooves above.

 **Centre Route**　　　　　**18m VD**

FA Jeremy Talbot & G. Jones 1959

Take the face, avoiding the bulge by stepping left at the top.

**Left Flake Corner**　　　　　**18m VD**

FA John Brailsford & St Athan MRT 1954

Climb the left corner of the raised slab on positive holds, finishing direct up the wall when the corner runs out.

**Central Flake**　　　　　**18m S 4a**

FA John Brailsford & St Athan MRT 1954

A classy line, with one of the best sinker wires you'll ever place. Climb the centre of the raised slab on cracks and juggy edges. A little polished in places.

**Flake Corner**　　　　　**18m VD**

FA John Brailsford & St Athan MRT 1954

Climb the right corner of the raised slab, finishing up the wall above.

**Right Edge**　　　　　**18m VD**

FA John Brailsford & St Athan MRT 1954

An intricate line that follows the right edge of the tor.

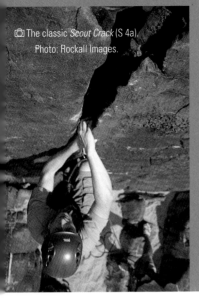

The classic *Scout Crack* (S 4a).
Photo: Rockall Images.

# LITTLE STAR WALL

This short wall with its vertical routes and good protection offers a handful of worthwhile climbs across the grades on solid rock, most notably the classic crackline *Scout Crack* and technical test piece *Super Direct*. The climbing is accessible about 4 hours either side of low water.

SS 5268 8778

**Aspect**: S

### ① Scout Crack                    12m S 4a

*FA John Brailsford & St Athan MRT 1954*

If you like crack climbs you'll love this route. Follow the wide crack from start to finish, avoiding the ledge on the left and the disgrace associated with touching it.

### ② Super Direct                    12m E1 5c

*FFA Jim Perrin & C. Tringham 1970*

A short technical test piece up the steep wall, with adequate protection and perfect rock. Head directly up the wall past the large pocket at half height.

### ③ Twinkle                    12m S 4a

*FA John Brailsford & St Athan MRT 1954*

This line wanders pleasantly across the wall, starting below the white quartz patch. Climb the crack and wall to the quartz, then traverse out right on good holds to finish in the wide crack. A VS 4c variant goes direct up the wall from the quartz patch.

### ④ Stella                    10m VS 4c

*FA John Brailsford & St Athan MRT 1954*

Head straight up the wall crossing *Twinkle* at half height.

### ⑤ Twin Crack Left                    9m VD

*FA John Brailsford & St Athan MRT 1954*

The left of the two cracks at the right end of the wall.

### ⑥ Twin Crack Right                    7m D

*FA John Brailsford & St Athan MRT 1954*

Short but pleasant, the right of the two cracks at the end of the wall.

📷 Chris 'Homer' Ledden and Rosie Dyer starting up the first pitch of the *East Ridge* (S). Photo: Matt Woodfield.

# GREAT TOR

This grand headland sits majestically between Oxwich Bay and Three Cliffs Bay, rising as a solid tower of limestone out of sea and sand. There are options to climb on every face of the tor, but the line of choice up the *East Ridge* provides you with four pitches of varied climbing, stunning scenery and Gower's longest route. Although non-tidal, the first pitch can be affected by rough seas. Descent from the summit is best made by scrambling off the worn path on the back (north side) of the tor, taking care down the polished gully.

SS 5297 8763

**Aspect**: S

Approach

*Cigdem + Ben Sept 2015*

**1  East Ridge**                                      **71m S**

*FA Alan Osborn & S. Osborn 1952*

The route begins from a flat non-tidal platform at the base of the east ridge of the tor. Belay ledges are large enough for a family picnic and escape is possible over easy ground to the right (east) for most of the route, making this the ideal local introduction to multi-pitch climbing. Pitches 2 and 3 can easily be linked together. Possible variations to the first two pitches are included, giving a grade of HS.

**1. 18m** Gain the crack in the middle of the wall from a line of good holds out left. Continue either up the steep rock, or step right to easier ground and continue to a large ledge to belay.

**1a. 18m 4b** Climb the twin finger cracks with interest to easy ground before the belay ledge.

**2. 16m** Step to the left and climb the groove in the end of the wall, continuing up the arête to another good ledge.

**2a. 16m 4b** Climb the crack in the middle of the wall above, past the smooth ledge at half height and up to the next large ledge.

**3. 13m** Continue up the arête to belay before the wall steepens.

**4. 24m** Follow the ridge up over ledges to belay on the summit. If you're British, now's the time to eat your sandwiches. Well done!

📷 Looking out from the cave on the Great Tor, found by traversing left when descending to the start of the route.

# ODIN'S WALL

Tucked away on the east side of the Great Tor, this crag boasts some of the best-quality rock around that rises straight out of the golden sand. It's slightly more remote location offers good climbing away from the crowds found at the more popular cliffs in the area. Odin's Wall offers a section of lower-grade routes, each with its own distinct character. This is a tidal crag and can be climbed about 2 hours either side of low water.

Odin himself, Norse god and father to Thor, has not recorded any of his own ascents here.

SS 5305 8771

**Aspect**: S

###  Left Corner and Crack       18m VS 4c
*FA Jeremy Talbot 1961*

Step up onto the rock arch and bridge up the corner to gain the large ledge. Step back right and finish up the cracks above.

### ❷ Cave Crack       20m HS 4b
*FA Roger Owen & Derrick Jones 1959*

Start up the corner but make a tricky traverse right before the ledge to gain the triangular cave. Continue rightwards and follow the diagonal crack to finish.

### ❸ Cave Crack Direct       19m VS 4b
*FA Jeremy Talbot 1959*

Follow *Cave Crack* to the cave, then head straight up the crack above to the top.

### ❹ Direct       18m VS 5a
*FA Jeremy Talbot & Donald Thomas 1959*

A bouldery lower section leads to an easier finish. A determined approach will work well at the start. Begin just to the right of the cave and climb powerfully past the bulge to gain the upper cracks.

A typical day climbing at Tor Bay with Dan Harris on *Stella* (VS 4C). Photo: Stuart Llewellyn.

Charles Romijn.

### ⑤ Fiechtl                                            18m S

*FA Jeremy Talbot & Donald Thomas 1959*

Begin at a niche on the right side of the wall. Climb up and right into the wide crack, then break out left and follow cracks and good holds to the top.

### ⑥ Wide Crack                                        18m D

*FA Roger Owen & Derrick Jones 1959*

Start as for *Fiechtl*, but continue up the awkward crack and finish up the corner above.

Nick Foulds heading into the darkness of
*Under Milk Wood* (VS 4b).
Photo: Matt Woodfield.

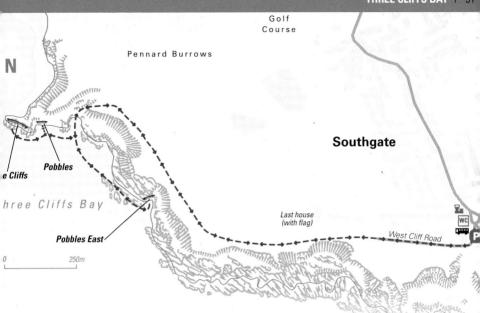

# THREE CLIFFS BAY

With its meandering river, idyllic castle ruins and miles of endless sand, Three Cliffs Bay provides one of the most picturesque climbing locations in the country. The Three Cliffs themselves are a protrusion of light-grey limestone rising straight out of yellow sand. The river runs past its western side and a large cave cuts through the heart of the crag. Although tidal, these cliffs are not a serious undertaking and provide some fantastic low- to mid-grade routes, great views and a lovely spot for a picnic.

**Approach**: Park in Southgate in the car park just over the roundabout at the end of the village; a small fee helps the National Trust to keep the area special. Toilets and a café/shop are on standby to meet your pre-climbing needs. Once you're ready to start your day, follow the private road right (West Cliff Road) moving onto one of the many footpaths when it runs out. Keep going for about 10 minutes until looking down on the bay itself, then head right and down sand dune and rocky steps onto the beach (about 20 minutes in total).

**Three Cliffs** and **Pobbles**: just a couple of minutes walk to the right across the beach.

**Pobbles East**: a couple of minutes walk to the left. Walk past the small headland with its long ledges and Pobbles East is tucked into a small cove at its end, before the main headland begins.

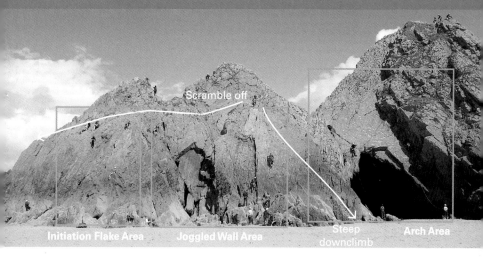

Scramble off

Steep downclimb

Initiation Flake Area    Joggled Wall Area    Arch Area

# THREE CLIFFS

This area is characterised by a wealth of easy, slabby and pleasant routes, the perfect place for your first climbs as it was for the thousands who came before you. You do have to scratch around for good gear for belays at the top, but it is there somewhere. The best descent is to scramble off to the left (when facing the crag) and down a series of steps. The beach is rarely quiet and those climbing on the cliffs are likely to be a main attraction. The climbing is accessible about 3 hours either side of low water.

## INITIATION FLAKE AREA

SS 5378 8777

**Aspect**: S

**Wall Climb 1**                    **9m D**

*FA John Brailsford & St Athan MRT 1954/55*

Climb the wall left of the gaping hole.

**Cleft 1**                         **10m D**

*FA John Brailsford & St Athan MRT 1954/55*

Bridge up the cleft until it narrows; finish up the wall above.

The frequently photographed Three Cliffs Bay.
Photo: Wayne Tucker

### Wall Climb 2　　　　　　　　　　　10m D
*FA John Brailsford & St Athan MRT 1954/55*

Head straight up the wall between the two clefts.

### Cleft 2　　　　　　　　　　　　　11m VD
*FA John Brailsford & St Athan MRT 1954/55*

Climb the right-hand cleft, keeping left past the protruding block near the top.

### Left Corner　　　　　　　　　　　11m M
*FA John Brailsford & St Athan MRT 1954/55*

Climb the corner on the left side of the raised slab on good holds.

Cigdem - Sept 2015

### Initiation Flake　　　　　　　　　12m S
*FA John Brailsford & St Athan MRT 1954/55*

A right of passage? Climb with style up the middle of the raised slab.

### Right Corner　　　　　　　　　　12m D
*FA John Brailsford & St Athan MRT 1954/55*

Climb the corner to the right of the raised slab on good holds.

### Meander　　　　　　　　　　　　12m D
*FA John Brailsford & St Athan MRT 1954/55*

Climb the slab to the ridge, finish up this.

Dan Lane climbing at Three Cliffs at the first BMC Gower Climbing Festival. Photo: Norman Gilman

## JOGGLED WALL AREA

This is the middle cliff of the three, offering a range of slabby routes from Diff to HVS. The main events here are the bold challenge of *Inverted V* and the ever popular *Joggled Wall*. Descent from the belays is easiest to the left (when facing the crag) and down large steps, or to the right and down the gully of your choice.

SS 5379 8777

**Aspect**: S

### ① Left Corner 2     16m VD

*FA John Brailsford & St Athan MRT 1954/55*

A tricky start leads to easier climbing above. Bridge up the corner and step onto the slab, following the corner to the top.

### ② Inverted V     16m HVS 4c

*FFA Roger Owen & C. Edwards 1959*

A bold route with enough protection where you need it, if you can find it. Climb the centre of the technical slab to the inverted 'V' in the overhang. Pull through this with relative ease to finish up the slab above.

It was John Brailsford and the St Athan MRT who first climbed these cliffs. In 1961 he created the first ever purpose-designed nut: the Acorn. It was the first time that something had been manufactured specifically for the job.

Cigdem - Sept 2016 + Ben

### ③ Spouse Crack     16m S 4a

*FA John Brailsford & St Athan MRT 1954/55*

Climb the crack running rightwards across the slab, move over the overhang to good holds in a groove. Finish up this groove, or up the cracks going leftwards.

### ④ Quartz Corner     16m HS 4b

*FA John Brailsford & St Athan MRT 1954/55*

Climb up the slim slab, moving right and through a steep crack at the white quartz. Follow this crack to the top.

### ⑤ Joggled Wall     18m VD

*FA John Brailsford & St Athan MRT 1954/55*

A popular route that climbs the brown slab left of the small corner. Follow this on good holds to the overhang above, dodge left round the hard bit and follow the shallow corner above to the top.

### ⑥ Joggled Wall Direct     17m HS 4a

*FA C. Edwards & Roger Owen, Chris Andrews 1959*

As for *Joggled Wall*, but tackles the overhang directly.

📷 Nick Foulds enjoying a beautiful day at the beach on *Joggled Wall Direct* (HS 4a). Photo: Matt Woodfield.

**Left Edge**          **17m HS 4b**

*FA C. Edwards, Roger Owen, Chris Andrews 1959*

Climb the left edge of the raised slab on shiny rock.

 **Perseverance**          **18m HS 4b**

*FA John Brailsford & St Athan MRT 1954/55*

Follow cracks up the middle of the slab on small holds but with good gear. *Ben Sept 2015*

## ARCH AREA

The rock surrounding the cave through the cliff provides some of the harder and more exciting routes in the bay. Belays for *Arch Slab* and *Scavenger* rely on the old peg being backed up with some good hard-to-find wires.
SS 5379 8778

**Aspect**: S

**1 Arch Slab**          **24m VS 4c**

*FA Roger Owen, C. Edwards & Chris Andrews 1959*

Follow the groove on the left side of the cave to a niche below the leftwards-rising break. Traverse rightwards to a good hold, then bridge to an exposed position above the apex of the through cave. Glance downwards for the full experience, then finish direct up the slab on small cracks.

**2 Under Milk Wood**          **21m VS 4b**

*FA R. McElliot & Richard Hoare 1984*

An entertaining and enjoyable route where size really does matter. Inside the through cave on the left is an easy slab; follow this up to black rock above and a good thread. Bridge up the groove on good holds until the angle eases and the cave closes in. From here struggle towards the light of your subterranean exit or make your retreat from good threads, leaving this challenge for someone of a 'smaller frame'. Helmets may need to be pushed in front of you on this final section; large gear and excess clothing is not advised.

**3 Scavenger**          **26m VS 4c**

*FA John Brailsford & St Athan MRT 1954/55*

Quite a popular route (evident by the level of polish at every step), but still a hugely enjoyable climb. Gain and follow the corner up the slab to finish on the ledge. Can be very slippery when wet.

# POBBLES

This small slabby crag sits just to the east of the main climbing area and provides some good easier climbs away from the crowds. The area is also further up the beach than Three Cliffs, allowing for a few more routes to be bagged as the tide races in. The crag is accessible about 4 hours either side of low water.

SS 5387 8777

**Aspect**: S

**1 Gwyn's Route**                          **11m VS 5a**

*FA Swansea University Mountaineering Club 1973*

A popular well-protected problem, with the crux getting off the floor. A boulder problem start leads to a big rockover past the next overhang. The final overhang is taken direct, with some good hidden holds over the lip.

**2 Central Slab**                          **11m S 4a**

*FA Unknown*

Step through the overlap and follow cracks leftwards to finish.

**3 Left Corner**                          **11m VD**

*FA John Brailsford & St Athan MRT 1954/55*

Gain the corner from the left and climb while making use of the shattered crack to the side.

**4 Left Pillar**                          **11m VD**

*FA John Brailsford & St Athan MRT 1954/55*

Climb the left side of the raised slab on good holds.

**5 Pillar Route**                          **11m D**

*FA John Brailsford & St Athan MRT 1954/55*

Follow cracks up the centre of the slab, past a useful protruding block.

**6 Right Edge**                          **12m M**

*FA John Brailsford & St Athan MRT 1954/55*

Scramble up to and climb the right edge of the slab.

# POBBLES EAST

This crag sets itself away from the crowds and polished classics in its own private cove. The climbing is surprisingly good once you get past the barnacle line, with some real hidden gems to find.

Descents are best made by walking left (when facing the crag) and scrambling down where the angle eases. The climbing is accessible about 2 hours either side of low water, although the approach gets cut off before the crag gets wet so keep an eye on the incoming tide.

SS 5425 8753

**Aspect**: SE

**1 The Groove**                          **12m M**

*FA John Brailsford & St Athan MRT 1954/55*

This line provides good well-protected climbing up the groove to the left of the main slab.

**2 Slab Route**                          **12m S**

*FA John Brailsford & St Athan MRT 1954/55*

Start up the corner on the left of the slab until a move right at a large slot can be made; finish up the slab.

### 3 Limpet Route      12m VS 5b
*FA John Brailsford & St Athan MRT 1954/55*

An almost desperate start on the smooth slab leads to much easier ground above. Protection arrives when it's no longer needed.

### 4 Barnacle Bulge      12m VS 4c
*FA John Brailsford & St Athan MRT 1954/55*

A difficult bouldery start leads to an easy finish; the position of limpets can affect the grade. Gain the arête from the capped groove below.

### 5 Smalt      14m VS 4c
*FA Goi Ashmore 20th February 1999*

A fantastic line following the obvious crack up the wall. Gain the base of the crack with interest, then follow it past good moves and good gear to the top.

### 6 Blue Grass      14m HVS 4c
*FA Goi Ashmore 20th February 1999*

A bold undertaking following the line of weakness up the wall. An athletic rockover leads into a washed groove that is followed to more featured rock and protection. Finish direct up the wall above.

Mike Griffiths on *Limpet Route* (VS 5b). Photo: Matt Woodfield.

### 7 Corner Groove      14m D
*FA John Brailsford & St Athan MRT 1954/55*

A pleasant route that does as the name suggests: climbs the corner groove to the top.

### 8 Twin Crack Slab      14m M
*FA John Brailsford & St Athan MRT 1954/55*

Follow the cracks up the wall passing numerous holes en route.

### 9 Jagged Edge      14m VD
*FA John Brailsford & St Athan MRT 1954/55*

Follow the right edge of the wall on rough rock.

Cai Bishop-Guest making the clip on *Goose in Lucy* (F6c).
Photo: Make The Next Move Images.

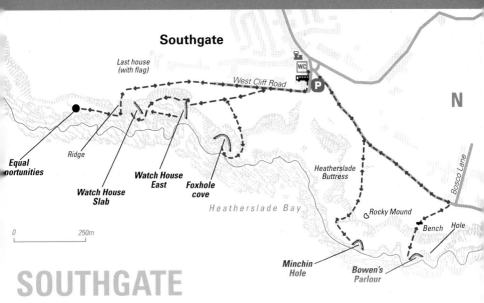

# SOUTHGATE

Spread over several excellent venues, Southgate has the best selection of sport climbs on Gower. Climbs range from fantastic entry-level climbs to the hardest sport route on Gower, reported at 8b. If clipping bolts is your thing this is the area to visit. You may find yourself starting your day at one crag before visiting several other venues, particularly if the tides are right to take advantage of the short-distance crag-hopping on offer. To finish your day off there are two coffee shops next to the parking and a pub along the main road.

**Approach**: Drive to Southgate and park in the car park beyond the roundabout for a small fee (or for free if you're a member of the National Trust). The car park is perched above the small beach of Heatherslade Bay. The approaches to the crags are split into east and west (left and right, respectively, when looking out to sea) when leaving the car park.

**West of Heatherslade Bay**

**Equal Opportunities:** Leave the car park and go right (looking out to sea) along West Cliff Road. Continue onto the coastal path towards the last house (usually flying a flag). Where the path splits with a bridleway, head left along the path then down left alongside a striking ridge of rock. At the notch in the ridge, cross to the other side

and follow down grass and rocky ledges to a small cave with a grassy base.

For all three sport venues described below, leave the car park and head right (looking out to sea) along West Cliff Road. After around 150m (before reaching house No. 8) bear left towards the coast. The headland is made up of two mounds separated by a lull in the middle.

**Watch House Slab:** Walk towards the second mound. Down and right of this is a track cut back from gorse bushes which weaves down the slope. Following this brings you down to a rocky platform; scramble right around the corner into a non-tidal zawn.

**Watch House East:** As for Watch House Slab, but walk left from the rocky platform to the steep crag of Watch House East.

Fin of rock

Scary hole

Bowen's Parlour
approach

**Foxhole Cove:** Walk down the left side of the first mound and follow the vague scree slope steeply downwards. As the terrain becomes rocky and slightly more solid (after about 50m), bear right until you drop down and reach the cove.

### East of Heatherslade Bay

A buttress of rock below and left of the car park overlooks the bay and is known as Heatherslade Buttress. Leave the car park leftwards (looking out to sea) heading along East Cliff Road.

**Minchin Hole:** Head towards the highest rocky mound visible beyond Heatherslade Buttress. Once at this mound take a footpath down and bearing left around its side just above the high tide level. Keep scrambling along the coast until the very obvious entrance is reached.

**Bowen's Parlour:** Stay on East Cliff Road until you reach Bosco Lane on your left. At this point strike diagonally right towards the sea to reach a lone bench. From here head straight down to the coast. The crag is identified by a central fin of rock down the middle of the zawn. The descent into the crag is on the right and is slightly insecure underfoot.

**Access agreements:** Southgate is a complex stretch of coastline with some very important sites. As such there are a few restrictions and guidelines that climbers must follow. If you plan on climbing at Minchin Hole, please read the detailed points at the beginning of that section. At Bacon Hole it's quite simple: there is a complete climbing ban due to geological importance and nesting bats. For further information search the BMC's Regional Access Database for these and other surrounding sites not covered in this guidebook.

Equal Opportunities
approach

Chris Allen Jr bouldering
at Equal Opportunities
Photo: Matt Woodfield

# EQUAL OPPORTUNITIES

This small bouldering venue, set in a beautiful sheltered
suntrap, uses the steep right wall of a small cave to
give the burliest problems on the peninsular. The steep
wall dries quickly, but the kick plate at the base seeps
badly after rain. The landings are grassy, but a layer of
hard sandstone lies just under the surface so a mat is
worthwhile. The area is easily identified by the large
amount of graffiti on the walls of the cave.

SS 5455 8731

**Aspect**: S

# WATCH HOUSE SLAB

Transformed a few years ago, this pleasant crag sports a collection of welcoming slabby bolted routes and some steeper outings. The angle may be inviting but don't be fooled; some of these lines require technical wizardry. The crag receives afternoon sun and is in a very sheltered location. It dries quickly after rain, apart from the odd wet streak underneath the bulges on the right of the crag. For a full day out, start here then head across to the other side of the rocky platform for the steeper Watch House East crag.

SS 5478 8730

**Aspect**: SW

**① Excavation**                    **12m F5**

*FA John Bullock & Danny McCarroll 2008*

Begin up the honeycomb feature past a rib where the terrain steepens and your footwork comes into play. An F6a variation can be climbed, keeping left of the bolts at all times.

**② Tickety-Boo**                    **11m F5+**

*FA John Bullock & Danny McCarroll 2008*

Start on honeycomb holds, passing an awkward overlap at halfway. A little cracker.

**③ Sport Wars**                    **12m F6a**

*FA Dan Cook & Danny McCarroll 2008*

A terrific climb. Gain the first bolt from the left moving onto good holds, rocking over leads to just below an overlap. Continue upwards on good holds.

**④ Tread Gently**                    **12m F6b+**

*FA John Bullock & Danny McCarroll 2008*

Fiendishly thin and difficult climbing at the start, which then gives way to easier ground above.

**⑤ St Vitus' Dance**                    **13m F6c+**

*FA Danny McCarroll & Dan Cook 2008*

Dance your way up the white-streaked wall. Technical and with incredibly small holds (if you can call them that).

📷 Amy Romijn cruising up *Sport Wars* (F6a). Photo: Stuart Llewellyn.

# WATCH HOUSE EAST

A much steeper affair than its sister crag, Watch House East is home to mostly high 6s and low 7s. It is possible to climb the left-hand routes with the tide in, but in general avoid climbing for 2 hours either side of high tide. The crag receives the sun early afternoon and the far right routes closest to the sea will need a prolonged dry, warm spell for the holds to be in condition.
SS 5494 8731

**Aspect**: SW

**① Left Wing Rebolt**                               **13m F6b**

*FA Danny McCarroll & John Bullock 2009*

Hard moves from the floor (especially for shorties) lead onto good holds. The first two bolts are shared with *Straining Pitch*. Follow a diagonal break leftwards on good holds before moving into some blind territory before the lower off.

**② Straining Pitch**                                **18m F6b**

*FA John Bullock & Gwyn Evans 1989*

A stunning, steep route starting from the crystal finger rail. Make moves onto good red jugs, before steps rightwards take you beneath an overhanging crack. Climb this into a small niche. The angle eases allowing for a rest before blind but easy climbing over the roof. Slightly harder than *Left Wing Rebolt*.

**③ Touch and Go**                                   **18m F7a+**

*FA Danny McCarroll & John Bullock October 2010*

Shares the same start and first bolt as *Jump to Conclusions*. Head left along the large crystallised break before making moves up the impeding headwall. Flat holds bring you into a blocky section and a belay on a short slab.

**④ Jump to Conclusions**                            **18m F7a**

*FA John Bullock & Martyn Kydd 2nd September 1989*

This takes a more direct line through the overhanging terrain making a dyno to a jug up and left, through the red and white crystal band. Follow the leaning wall above to a ledge and follow a rib.

**⑥ The Drilling Fields**                            **16m F7a**

*FA John Bullock & Danny McCarroll 2008*

Another slab master class on small holds before juggy endings.

**⑦ Anonymous Bosch**                               **12m F6b**

*FA John Bullock & Danny McCarroll 2008*

Use the overlapping flakes to get to the sections of upper bulges onto some thin moves out left before heading right over the second bulge. Very good.

**⑧ Jaded Locals**                                   **12m F6b+**

*FA John Bullock & Danny McCarroll 2008*

Begin as for *Anonymous Bosch*. At the second bolt take the right-hand line, presenting some fine steep climbing through the overlaps.

**⑨ I Bolt, Therefore I Am**                         **13m F6c+**

*FA John Bullock & Danny McCarroll 2008*

Balancy and technical for the first half, then crimpy and thin past the bulge to the belay. Lacks independence from neighbouring lines but is very worthwhile.

**⑩ Trad Man**                                       **15m F6a+**

*FA John Bullock & Danny McCarroll 2008*

A delicate approach at the start is needed. Don't get sucked into the white crystallised wall; make moves right to gain the upper section which can feel insecure.

### 5 Pump Action       20m F7a+

*FA John Bullock & Roy Thomas 1989*

The steep blunt arête to the left of the distinct red groove. Begin at bands of red and white crystal ledges before making your way up a vague arête. Use undercuts where the rock steepens, before the angle changes drastically following a broken corner to the shared belay with *Nia Miss*.

### 6 Clip Joint       19m F6c

*FA John Bullock & Gwyn Evans 16th May 1989*

A good route that ends all too soon. Take the red overhanging groove with mostly big holds with increased difficulty to a good incut slot. The slab above leads to moves on an arête to a belay that might just be out of reach.

### 7 No Rest for the Wicked       9m F7a

*FA Adrian Berry 1995*

Clipstick useful for the first high bolt. Follow the colourful bulbous overhanging feature, using a shared bolt with *Too Many Fingers* and its mixed belay. Starting by step-ping off the boulder is cheating and not F7a. Alternatively, *Nia Miss* or *Clip Joint* can be used as a finish.

### 8 Too Many Fingers (Danny's Boy)       10m F7a

*FA Danny McCarroll & John Bullock 2008*

A short pumpy route taking the leaning wall on the right side of the crag. Step off the large boulder and lower off just after turning the roof at a tat belay, or finish up *Nia Miss* or *Clip Joint*. Can be climbed on the right side at a grade easier.

### 9 Nia Miss       20m F5+

*FA John Bullock & Danny McCarroll 2008*

An adventurous sport route (if such a thing exists). Scramble up the right side of the crag to an anchor bolt which is for belaying on the ledge. Long extenders are worthwhile to reduce the rope drag. Step immediately leftwards across the slab, finishing up a broken corner to a lower off. An alternative, harder finish takes the blunt arête of *Clip Joint*.

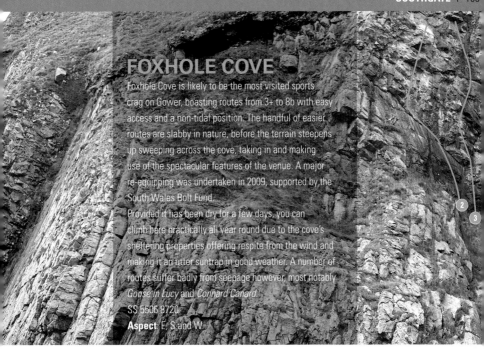

# FOXHOLE COVE

Foxhole Cove is likely to be the most visited sports crag on Gower, boasting routes from 3+ to 8b with easy access and a non-tidal position. The handful of easier routes are slabby in nature, before the terrain steepens up sweeping across the cove, taking in and making use of the spectacular features of the venue. A major re-equipping was undertaken in 2009, supported by the South Wales Bolt Fund.

Provided it has been dry for a few days, you can climb here practically all year round due to the cove's sheltering properties offering respite from the wind and making it an utter suntrap in good weather. A number of routes suffer badly from seepage however, most notably *Goose in Lucy* and *Connard Canard*.

SS 5506 8720
**Aspect**: E, S and W

### ① The Power of the Leopard Skin Leg Warmers 13m F3+

*FA Rhoslyn Frugtniet March 2010*

A pleasurable outing on superb friction that has quickly become popular. Head towards the sea down a channel below the main crag. Bear right into a zawn for a route on its own.

### ② Never Out-Fox the Fox      12m F5

*FA Stuart Llewellyn 10th June 2010*

Start on the grass bank and move left onto the black slab, where small holds allow progress higher into a large break. With the delicacies over, start yarding on massive holds to reach a pedestal. Use some crafty out-of-sight holds to reach the distant lower off.

### ③ Cunning Little Fox      12m F5

*FA Stuart Llewellyn 25th May 2010*

You'll need a cunning plan, perhaps as cunning as a fox who's just been appointed Professor of Cunning at Oxford University. Bridge up the short wall and tend leftwards into a sweep, before rocking over onto the rightward-facing ramp. Make some balancey moves on the slab while trying to find suitable holds to progress to the lower off.

Simon Rawlinson shooting through Pump Action (F7a+).
Photo: Rob Lamey

### 4 Unlikely Alliance — 13m F6a+

*FA John Bullock 2002*

The first few moves can feel a little stiff and blind, but good solid wall climbing awaits you. Can be climbed several different ways, resulting in a grade from F5+ to about F6b the further right you go. Rarely straightforward.

### 5 Connard Canard — 12m F7a+

*FA Gary Gibson 1st September 1998*

Distinctly sequencey and difficult to onsight. Climbing left and using a series of rockovers gives the suggested grade; keeping a line on the right probably increases the grade to 7b. The lower off is just out of sight above the conglomerate ledge.

### 6 Goose in Lucy — 12m F6c

*FA Roy Thomas & Simon Coles 11th May 1996*

A Foxhole favourite. Start from the hump using finger pockets to a difficult second clip. Decisions, decisions; small crimps or jump to the good holds? Work left along the big shelf to gain the head wall into undercuts then throw for a generally juggy affair. A brilliant route! For an extra-long work out, move out across right at the belay and head up the broken corner to the top of the crag and tick off *Lucky Lizzy* 23m 6c+.

### 7 Surplomb de Ray — 23m F8b

*FA Simon Rawlinson 20th June 2010*

The hardest sport route on Gower. Climb straight through the overhang via a very hard bouldery sequence to eventually gain the tufa jug at the intermediate belay of *Pioneers of the Hypnotic Groove*. Continue all the way to the top of the crag to finish.

### 8 Pioneers of the Hypnotic Groove — 25m F7b

*FA Goi Ashmore & Simon Coles 19th April 1996*

Follows the eye-grabbing line towards the back of the cave. Head up to a shelf before blasting through fantastic terrain, where an ability to bridge is beneficial. The newest bolts are the thinnest. Like the previous two routes, continue past the first belay to the top of the crag for a fuller Foxhole experience.

### 9 Un-named — 11m F8a?

*FA Unknown*

This route is just left of the conglomerate floor, sharing the first and second bolts of *Palace of Swords Reversed*. The high bolts are in a bad condition but this route has been included here to avoid confusion with other lines. Has not been climbed since a crucial hold broke off, so the grade may be inaccurate.

### 10 Palace of Swords Reversed     11m F8a
*FA Goi Ashmore 8th September 1996*

Powerful climbing using small holds on seriously overhanging rock.

In the middle of the crag is a bulgy pillar left of a cave. The starts of the climbs on this pillar can be swapped with each other without much effect on grade.

### 11 Chicken Licken     8m F6c+
*FA Roy Thomas 19th July 1996*

Packs it all in over a short distance and very spicy! Good footwork is key. The upper sections of the next few routes can be done from the mid-height ledge. Linking this route with *Foxy Lady* gives *Foxy Chicken*, F7a+.

### 12 Foxy Lady     18m F7a
*FA John Bullock & Roy Thomas May 1990*

Head up the cracks in the middle of the pillar to gain the break. Pull out over the bulge to continue strenuously up layback flakes to the belay.

### 13 The Hooker     18m F7a
*FA John Bullock & Roy Thomas June 1990*

Gain the break via *Foxy Lady*'s start. Once on the slab take the right-hand line. Easy moves lead to the impending headwall and a tough crux to reach the lower off.

### 14 Joy de Viva     17m F7a
*FA Gary Gibson 5th July 1997*

An excellent route. Climb up to the small cave before launching out right for a good rail. Make some hard moves on some small features to progress higher where the angle increases (but luckily so do the holds).

### 15 Power Struggle     17m F7b+
*FA Martin Crocker & John Harwood 1st May 1994*

The original Foxhole sport route and one of the first to raise sport climbing standards on Gower. Share the same start as *Ducky Lucky*, then break out left where a fierce bouldering problem awaits. Bear left to finish to

*Staring up through the alluring Pioneers of the Hypnotic Groove (F7b). Photo: John Bullock.*

the lower off of *Joy de Viva*. Stepping right to the *Ducky Lucky* lower off drops the grade to 7b.

### 16 Ducky Lucky     14m F7a+
*FA Roy Thomas 10th August 1996*

Follow the crackline up to the recess and small cave. Make a move right onto good layback holds, before crimpy moves on sharp holds lead you to finishing jugs and the lower off.

### 17 The Day the Sky Fell In     14m F6b+
*FA Roy Thomas 18th May 1996*

Not a soft touch, this short journey gives a good workout. Utilise undercuts and slots to gain a good side pull and launch up to a good hold. The crux comes getting into a large layback and also exiting rightwards through the earthy bulge (take care: loose rock), before moving back left to the shared lower off.

Simon Robinson attempting to
*Jump the Sun* (F7a+).
Photo: Stuart Llewellyn.

# MINCHIN HOLE

Minchin Hole has a complex history for a relatively young crag. It was banned for climbing for nearly ten years but in 2010 local climbers and the BMC, working with the National Trust, resolved and lifted the ban. Climbers can now access this impressive gothic cathedral-like venue. The steep walls of Minchin provide a shaded alternative to the likes of Foxhole and Watch House East in the summer, as it doesn't get a lot of sun. It's virtually non-tidal, but keep an eye on the tide to ensure you can escape.

**Minchin Hole** is a large coastal fissure which has been studied for nearly a century. Remains of lions, spotted hyena, horse, wild boar and deer have been excavated from the site. The site is important to the overall understanding of the history of much of the Last Interglacial and early Last Cold Stage in the British Isles. It contains two raised beaches, representing two separate interglacial periods. The caves along this part of the coast, most notably Minchin Hole and Bacon Hole, contain the remains of a richly fossiliferous sequence which, to expert knowledge, has no parallel in Britain. We are talking here about deposits which date to the period between about 90,000 and 120,000 years ago.

### Access agreements

Minchin Hole is a Site of Special Scientific Interest (SSSI) and, as such, the following access agreement must be carefully adhered to.

The 'stuck-on' conglomerate features are particularly sensitive and important from a conservation perspective; they are also quite fragile and should be avoided. No loose rock is to be removed. Cave deposits go right up to the roof clinging to the sides outside as well as inside the cave. It is important that the complete sequence of rock is not disturbed.

Vegetation should be left alone. Gardening is not permitted and the cliff face must be left undisturbed.

Bolt replacement on existing routes is only allowed on a like-for-like basis.

No new developments are allowed due to the sensitive nature of the site.

Please avoid the loose flying buttress of debris left of the start of *Kestrel*. It is part of the bone-bearing 'cave earth' and has been left there to show how the sediments inside the cave link with those in the entrance.

Should you see any fossils or bones, do not dislodge if partially buried and please notify the National Trust on gower.admin@ nationaltrust.org.uk or telephone the office on 01792 390636. Previous guidebooks describe many other routes, but these should be left as part of the crag's history. Only the routes described here should be climbed. Please respect this and all the work that has gone into regaining access to this venue.

📷 Photo: Stefan Doerr.

The important flying buttress. Please avoid!

The first two routes are accessed by scrambling to a small terrace, where the belayer can clip themselves in. A clip stick is useful at this venue.

SS 5552 8686

**Aspect**: E and W

### ① Beyond the Fringe 10m F6b

*FA Roy Thomas 4th May 1998*

The first bolt is a little high. Begin up the slab passing a large conglomerate hold. Take on the surprisingly steep head wall on positive (if sometimes painful) holds.

### ② Triple Sigh 13m F6b+

*FA Roy Thomas 4th May 1998*

Takes a steep direct line up the rib on some snappy holds. Bear right on conglomerate holds towards the belay.

### ③ Jump the Sun 17m F7a+

*FA Roy Thomas 1st September 1998*

An excellent line which starts below the terrace of the first two lines. Initially pleasant slab climbing leads into vertical territory, before reaching through overlaps and some heart-in-mouth moves.

### ④ Crawling King Snake 22m F7b

*FA Gary Gibson 1999*

Further around again is a sweeping arête, with a ledge at the start. The quality of the line and condition of the bolts is unknown. The route has been included for completeness.

### ⑤ Kestrel 24m F7c+

*FA Tadas Nikonovas, date unknown*

Climbs the vague arête system to the lower off. Completely avoid the flying buttress of rock as it is of great importance (see access notes).

### ⑥ The Raven 23m F7a+

*FA Gary Gibson 25th May 1998*

The crag classic and a jug fest for most of the route until exiting the top of the crack system. Start at a 'V' feature, making moves through conglomerate bands before entering the finger crack system. Considered by some as the best route in South Wales at this grade.

# BOWEN'S PARLOUR

The parlour is a recent development with some excellent routes, often being compared to Foxhole if a little more compact. You'll soon discover the steepness of the upper cave area and how deceptive it is.

The venue is normally sheltered from the wind and tends to get the sun most of the day. The upper section is also sheltered from light rain, meaning climbing is still possible in light showers. It may be greasy during a warm spell due to its proximity to the sea.

The parlour has an upper and lower tier, the lower being accessible approximately 1 hour 30 mins either side of low tide. Walk down with the tide out or abseil into the zawn, but keep your eye on the tide as it will catch up with you quickly. Either climb out of one of the routes, or a slippery scramble can be made up the smooth ramp at the back to the upper tier (emphasis on the slippery).

## UPPER CAVE

SS 5571 8682

**Aspect**: S

**① Rudaceous Ramble**      **12m F6a+**

*FA John Bullock & Danny McCarroll 2009*

Climb up the groove making use of some breccia holds onto a ledge made of the same matter. Gain the crack above, and finish steeply to the belay. It's more solid than it appears, but helmets are advised.

**② Breccial Motion**      **11m F6b+**

*FA John Bullock & Danny McCarroll 2009*

As for *Rudaceous Ramble*, but at the ledge make moves right and climb the brilliant finish of *Parlour Games*. A very worthwhile linkup.

**③ Parlour Games**      **11m F7a+**

*FA Danny McCarroll & John Bullock 2010*

Climb the overhanging headwall, which is powerful and sustained.

**④ Parlour Français**      **12m F7c**

*FA Martin Richards & Andy Sharp 2010*

Begin up *Parlour Games* but take the right-hand steepening line through the bulge.

### 5 Spider        8m F6b+

*FA John Bullock & Danny McCarroll 2009*

The short arête is a worthwhile outing. Avoid if greasy.

### 6 Fly        8m F6b

*FA Danny McCarroll & John Bullock 2009*

Wall climbing using strange rock formations. Avoid using the impressive roof as it's difficult to get back on route.

### 7 Still Nifty at Fifty        8m F7a

*FA Danny McCarroll 13th November 2011*

Sandstone jugs lead to the base of the leaning pillar. This is climbed on good holds, which unfortunately run out. Move left and climb the very overhanging wall to a lower off at the apex of the roof.

### 8 When I'm 64        12m F7a

*FA John Bullock & Danny McCarroll 2010*

An inspiring route, considering it received its name from the age of the first ascensionist. Follows the steepening diagonal line rightwards to a 'brick' hold before finishing very steeply.

To access the next few routes, it's usual to get the leader to traverse over using the low bolts to protect the exposed position.

### 9 Aspidistra        10m F6b

*FA John Bullock & Danny McCarroll 2009*

At the top end of the grade, using a high undercut (difficult to use if short) to gain the steeper jugs. Shares a belay with *When I'm 64*.

### 10 Maud        10m F6b

*FA Danny McCarroll & John Bullock 2010*

From the ledge ascend the wall where good holds await you through the steep finale. Some loose rock.

## LOWER ZAWN

SS 5572 8680

**Aspect**: W

### 11 All of a Quiver        9m F6a

*FA Roy Thomas July 2010*

Begin at the back of the slippery slope. Endure sharp holds on the just off-vertical wall, before the niche brings the finale. This route shares a lower off with *Bowen Arrow*.

**12** **Bowen Arrow** **12m F6a**

FA Danny McCarroll & John Bullock 2010

Starts at the edge of the slope, taking good holds up the flakes and corner.

**13** **Reaction Series** **12m F6b**

FA Danny McCarroll & John Bullock 2010

Climb the corner to a massive ledge then veer left through overlaps. The holds are nice and big apart from the last few moves at the top.

**14** **Bowen to the Inevitable** **13m F6a**

FA John Bullock & Danny McCarroll 2010

Excellent natural climbing up the corner, making steep pulls through the apex of a small roof.

**15** **Parlour Vous le Sport** **13m F6a+**

FA Danny McCarroll & John Bullock 2010

Sharp climbing on the dimpled wall leads to a weave through the shield before punching through the small roof.

**16** **Feud for Thought** **13m F6b**

FA John Bullock & Danny McCarroll 2010

Positive holds throughout, except when the line has not had the opportunity to dry out (when it feels a grade harder). Delicate footwork and balance is a must.

**17** **Gentlemen Prefer Bolts** **13m F6c+**

FA John Bullock & Danny McCarroll 2010

Unrelenting, with a reachy start and some hard clips. The second half maintains its challenges.

**18** **Gentlemen's Relish** **13m F6a**

FA Roy Thomas & Goi Ashmore 2010

Pleasant corner climbing until the top, where thin hard moves make you work for the end.

**19** **Gentlemen's Retreat** **12m F6a+**

FA Roy Thomas & Dai Emmanuel 10th October 2010

There is no lower off for this route. Top out onto the

©Chris Shepherd beginning the crux sequence of *When I'm 64* (F7a) Photo: Stuart Llewellyn.

slanting ledge and use a hanger anchor to bring your second up, cleaning your gear. Walk off down the slant- ing ledge with the tide out. A clip stick is useful to avoid the potential soaking when trying the hard initial moves. Good technical climbing on difficult-to-read features.

## MORNING WALL

SS 5571 8680

**Aspect**: E

**20** **Wisdom of Age** **11m F5**

FA Danny McCarroll & John Bullock 2010

Gain the good low break off slopey holds, with the test low down before an enjoyable upper section. Shared lower off with *Sallies of Youth*.

**21** **Sallies of Youth** **11m F5**

FA Danny McCarroll & John Bullock 2010

Start further up the slope and move to the large ledge and cave with difficulties or some contortionist trickery. Climb more logically up the heavily featured wall.

Ben Tiffin below the third and final roof of *Skive Direct* (HVS 5b). Photo: Stuart Llewellyn.

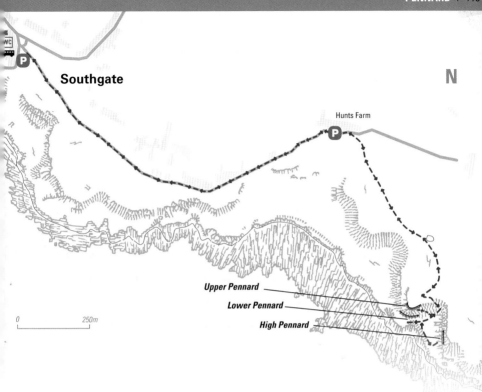

# PENNARD

The Pennard cliffs offer three different crags, all unaffected by the sea and just a short drive from Swansea with a short walk in. There is a good range of grades for all climbers offering some pleasant easy climbs, but is best suited to the HVS–E3 climber. The rock is mostly solid, but the tops are often loose and care should be taken when topping out. With the walls facing east, south and west, there's always an option to climb in the sun or shade.

**Approach**: Head past the National Trust car park in Southgate along the lane heading east, parking considerately outside Hunts Farm. The walk in takes about 15 minutes from here. From the farm follow the coastal path that runs east, down the valley and back up the other side, past the small pond and onto the brow of the hill. From the top of the hill walk out seawards along the headland until a path can be followed down on the left. **High Pennard** is visible in front of you as you descend, **Upper Pennard** appears to your right and **Lower Pennard** is underneath this (just follow the path around).

# LOWER PENNARD

This long wall lacks the height of the surrounding crags, but its routes are filled with technical interest giving good value for money. These are the easier routes of the area, but still offer a real challenge. The rock is compact on the face, but it can take a while to scratch around for good belays on the top.

SS 5671 8655

**Aspect**: S

belay and second pitch can be difficult to find from the base, so have a look before you begin. Start at the foot of the buttress by the large boulder.

**1. 18m 4c** Climb the wall to the corner, moving past the overhang and onto the short wall that leads to a ledge. Belay here.

**2. 18m 5a** Move right from the belay and then head up the wall above to a ledge. The final corner crack offers a great finish.

### 1 Alpha                                           36m HVS 5a

*FA Harold Insley et al. 1958*

This two-pitch route heads up the full height of the crag, with climbing that improves on the second pitch. The

### 2 Beta                                              16m VD

*FA Harold Insley et al. 1958*

Not particularly easy to protect and care should be taken with the rock. Follow the diagonal fault that splits the crag, finishing rightwards from the niche.

### 3 Beta Plus                                        14m HS 4b

*FA Robert Griffiths & Eryl Pardoe June 1966*

Climb the corner with interest. Continue past the peg to the capping overhang, which can be taken on its left or right.

### 4 Knucklefluster                                    11m E2 5c

*FA Andy Sharp & Pete Lewis 1984*

Steep and technical with good but spaced gear. Climb up into the groove and make a step out right to a good hold and thread. Head up to the break, then either step left and finish up *Beta Plus* or go direct up the steep ground above to finish.

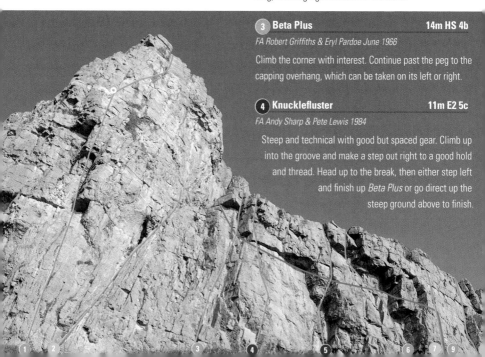

 Mike Griffiths warming up on *Beta* (VD). Photo: Matt Woodfield.

 **Gamma Minus**    **12m E1 5b**

*FA Eryl Pardoe & Robert Griffiths 1967*

A good route with an interesting move at half height. Climb the corner until a move right onto the arête can be made; finish up this arête and the crack above.

**6** **Gamma**    **12m HVS 5b**

*FA Eryl Pardoe & Robert Griffiths 1966*

Good gear and tough climbing define this route. Work your way up the corner until a tricky move left leads to good holds and the roof above. Finish through the groove above on more good holds in an exposed position.

**7** **Delta**    **13m S 4b**

*FA Martyn Hogge & Jim Birch 1967*

Climb the groove in the steep wall, finishing just right of the ivy patch.

**8** **Delta Minus**    **12m D**

*FA Swansea University Mountaineering Club 1966*

Follow the easy corner and wall above.

**9** **Girdle Traverse**    **20m HVS 5a**

*FA Jon Williams & P. Kokelaar 1967*

Originally three pitches, this reduced version takes in the best of the climbing on offer. This long pitch moves around the arêtes and corners of the face, and care should be taken to avoid immobilising drag.

Start up *Delta* then traverse around the arête to the left and into the corner of *Gamma*. Make some moves tentatively left to the arête, then continue past the overhung corner and along the break. Where the ground eases, finish left past the small overhanging block.

Steve Warrington on *Dan Dare* (E2 5c), enjoying glorious Gower sunshine in mid-January. Photo: Stuart Llewellyn.

# UPPER PENNARD

Set just above the lower cliff, Upper Pennard offers some good extreme routes on quality steep rock. The top section of the crag should be treated with care, however.
SS 5674 9657

**Aspect**: SE

**1 Tom Tom**        **24m E2 5c**

*FA Paul Donnithorne & Emma Alsford 1988*

From the bush at the foot of the wall, climb to the ledge at the base of the high corner passing through two scoops on the way. From the ledge, finish up the right wall and arête.

**2 Dan Dare**        **21m E2 5c**

*FA John Bullock & Gwyn Evans 6th May 1982*

Simply the best route on the face. From the bush at the foot of the wall, step up to a scoop then move up and right into a niche. Now follow the groove (crux) to the break above, traverse left and finish up the final easy groove.

**3 Desperate Dan**        **26m E3 5c**

*FA John Bullock & Graham Royle 7th August 1984*

A tough proposition. Follow *Dan Dare* to the break, then traverse right until below the undercut flake, Struggle up to this, finishing up the groove.

**4 White Feather**        **21m E4 6a**

*FA Andy Sharp & Owen Jones 1986*

Climb the steep crack up the wall to the break, making use of the rocky ramp out right. Finish up the final groove passing two pegs on the way. It is also possible to finish to the left as for *Desperate Dan*, giving a slightly lower grade of E3.

**5 Timorous Tarzan**        **36m E1 5a**

*FA Pat Littlejohn & John Harwood 3rd October 1980*

A sustained and pumpy start leads to an unstable finish. Success will be found with a combination of force and care. Layback the steep crack to its end, then traverse right on uninspiring holds to finish up the groove above.

**6 Bald Eagle**        **24m E4 6a**

*FA Andy Sharp & John Harwood 15th April 1984*

This line takes the rib on the right side of the wall to the break at half height, then steps left to finish up the final groove passing two pegs on the way.

# HIGH PENNARD

Facing west, this crag catches the afternoon sun and offers better climbing than might be expected on first inspection. There is plenty of scope for the E2/E3 climber.
SS 5681 8648
**Aspect**: W

 **Loony Left**                                        **24m E2 5c**

*FA John Bullock & Louise Cain 7th June 1987*

Starting to the left of the front pillar of the crag, head directly up to the right side of the overlap above (Friend 1.5). Surmount this with a mixture of superhuman technique and a long reach. Finish over easier ground up the corner above.

**②  Sudan**                                             **24m E2 5c**

*FFA Pat Littlejohn & John Harwood 3rd October 1980*

This route climbs the front pillar of the crag, starting at its base. Head up to the overhang and pass it using the thin crack on the left (crux). Now move back rightwards onto the pillar once again and finish direct, taking a bold approach.

**③  Skive**                                            **24m HVS 5a**

*FA Robert Griffiths & Eryl Pardoe November 1966*

A great mid-section makes up for a scrappy start and finish. Begin below the obvious groove in the middle of the crag. Climb up and over the first two roofs. At the third roof traverse, head delicately left and finish with care.

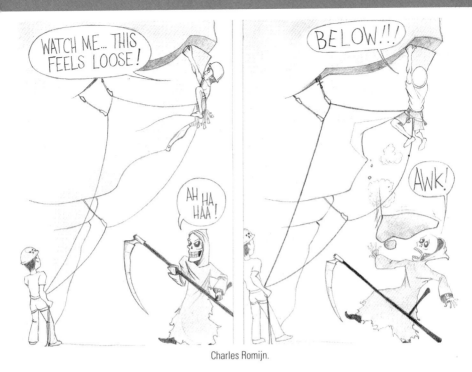

Charles Romijn.

**Skive Direct**  24m HVS 5b

*FA Robert Griffiths & J. Bayliss June 1967*

A better finish than its sister route, this line heads straight up from the right end of the final roof, following the groove with care to the top.

**Shogun**  24m E3 6a

*FA John Bullock & Gwyn Evans 15th September 1982*

Head straight up to the weakness in the overlap. Move with conviction past this and skirt out leftwards to the roof above. From here finish over easier ground up the groove, taking care with the rock.

**King Rat**  24m E3 6a

*FA Alun Richardson & Andy Long 1987*

A direct line with good climbing, starting as for *Shogun*. From the first overlap head straight up past the next and continue up the face past a thread to a break. Find and use the layback flake to finish.

**Samurai**  24m E3 6a

*FA John Bullock & Len Moran 2nd July 1986*

From the second overlap of *King Rat*, move right into the shallow groove and follow this past a small overhang and peg, finishing direct.

**Kensai/Phreatic Line Combination**  24m E3 5c

*FA John Bullock August 1986*

Begin below the obvious groove in the upper wall. The start is serious with small gear in suspect rock, but the rest of the route makes up for it. Climb the initial groove that leads to a rightward-trending overhang (good hidden wire), and then follow this until the horizontal break is met. Finish up the layback flake above you, heading leftwards.

**Seepage**  24m E1 5b

*FA Eryl Pardoe & C. Knight 1969*

On the right side of the crag is a ledge low down; climb to this, then directly up the wall above to a good thread. Step to the left and gain the groove to finish.

Simon Rawlinson nearing the end of *Fin* (F8a).
Photo: Adrian Berry.

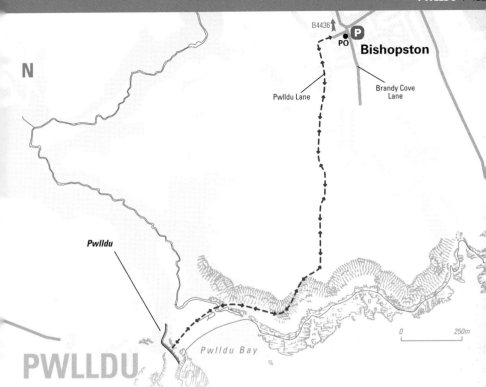

# PWLLDU

Although there are many contenders for tranquil and beautiful scenery on the peninsula, the small picturesque bay of Pwlldu may take the top prize. As you arrive at this secluded bay, you will be greeted with the sound of pebbles tumbling towards the sea from a dammed river. Pronounced 'pull-th-dee' and meaning Black Pool, the bay is unlikely to have the same crowds as neighbouring honey-pot beaches of Caswell and Langland.

The crag faces east and receives the sun until noon, making it a great morning venue. The routes are on the quarried faces and the climbing makes use of the square-cut features left over from the quarrying. A good selection of sport routes is available, and some may feel hard for the grade. The crag becomes coated with runoff from the banks at the top of the crag during wet spells, which can lead to a thin layer of mud flakes covering the rock. Once the crag is dry however, the climbing is very good.

**Approach**: Head to Bishopston along the B4436. If travelling east into Swansea, follow signposts for Bishopston. If heading west on the B4436 out of Swansea, Bishopston is not signposted. After passing a petrol station on your right, continue approximately half a mile downhill and take a left turn at the wide junction. Pass the Joiner's Arms pub and continue for around half a mile on Bishopston Road until it bends round sharply left near a Post Office (which sells snacks and drinks). Park on one of the side roads. Walk past the Post Office and head downhill, turning left down a lane (Pwlldu Lane). Walk down this lane (approximately 15 minutes), taking the right-hand gate at the end following the signpost for Pwlldu bay.

📷 *Illumination Arête*, with a characteristic Gower backdrop. Photo Simon Robinson.

Follow the uneven path, getting your first glimpse of this stunning secluded bay after about 5 minutes. Cross the beach, aiming for the middle of the quarried rock where a path can be picked up leading to the faces.

**Access agreements**: As Pwlldu is an SSSI, please keep your impact to a minimum. Take any litter home with you and stick to the main paths beneath the quarried walls. Use the bolt lower offs installed at the top of the climbs.

## PWLLDU BOULDERING

For the boulderer who wants to combine a session with a day at the beach without having the masses of onlookers as at Caswell, Pwlldu Bay has a small selection of blocks to play on. You probably won't make a full day out of the problems here, but that's probably due to the how sharp the rocks (or rather the barnacles) are. Head south from the quarried walls, where the horizon is dotted with blocks. Access to some of them is tidal, and the largest of the collection will need very low tides unless you're happy to get your pad wet. Over the brow of these boulders is another collection of rounded overhung arête problems into Bantam Bay.

Now a serene bay offering an escape from it all, the isolated natural harbour meant that Pwlldu was once a hive of smuggling activity. In the 18th century armed vessels smuggled tea and tobacco from Ireland and wine and brandy from France. From the bay, the contraband was carted through the Bishopston Valley woodlands up to surrounding farms. The house behind the pebble bank was the Beaufort Inn, and its cellars were used as storage. The landlord was rumoured to have a convenient arrangement with the smugglers, not always rolling out as many barrels as they had stored.

In the second half of the 19th century, smuggling was driven out by law enforcement officers and the illegal activities were replaced with farming, fishing and limestone quarrying. Lime was used extensively for whitewash and damp-proofing of houses, and the bay would be filled with ships waiting to export the rock to Devon. This thriving new industry brought in a second pub known as the Ship Inn. As this industry decayed, both inns lost their trade and eventually became private houses.

# PWLLDU

SS 5736 8699

**Aspect**: NE

## LEFT-HAND SIDE

### ① Swept Away      10m F6a+

*FA Roy Thomas & Phil Davies 2009*

Climbs the bulge and wall above to a shared lower off with *Clean Up*.

### ② Clean Up      10m F6a

*FA Myles Jordan & Roy Thomas 2009*

Crack climbing, usually out of condition from runoff.

### ③ Ashes to Ashes      18m F7a

*FA Roy Thomas & John Bullock October 1985*

A very good route climbing the open groove and cracks, with an out-of-character very hard last move.

### ④ Decades Apart      19m F6c

*FA Gary Gibson & Roy Thomas 2009*

A steep line with predominantly good holds following a line of leaning cracks. An excellent route to get warmed up on for the more difficult challenges in the area.

### ⑤ Forty for Three      10m F7b+

*FA Martin Crocker 10th July 1994*

Fingery off-balance face climbing on flat edges with sometimes difficult clips. Shares a widely spaced staple lower off with *Senser Part 1*.

### ⑥ Bellerophon      20m F7c+

*FA Martin Richards & Andy Sharp 7th August 2010*
*FA Simon Rawlinson 11th May 2008 (Chimera)*

A desperate continuation of a nails extension! Climb *Forty for Three* and continue up and left into the hanging groove (which was *Chimera* 7c). Continue up the steep rib slaying *Chimera* with *Bellerophon* on high.

### ⑦ Senser Part 1      10m F7b+

*FA Martin Crocker 24th July 1994*

Steady moves on this short route can be done statically, but are often lunged.

### ⑧ Senser      20m F7c+

*FA Martin Crocker 24th July 1994*

One of the original and best hard sport routes of South Wales. This route was the first claimed 8a in the area, which has since been downgraded. An excellently sustained route. Climb *Senser Part 1* and then make use

of side pulls and heel hooks before sloping off right via undercuts. Shared lower off with *Jezebel*.

### 9 Jezebel — 20m F7a+

*FA Martin Crocker 9th July 1994*

A line for technicians with a good sense of balance. Begin with a steep start, leading to a blunt prow and upper crack which can easily be wrong handed.

### 10 Crock Block — 10m F6c

*FA Roy Thomas July 1994*

A pumpy steep route, which relies on a worryingly large jammed block. You have been warned!

### 11 Old Slapper — 10m F7a+

*FA Roy Thomas 1994*

Repeatedly slap your way up the block; one for the boulderer within.

### 12 Skedaddle — 10m F7a+

*FA Martin Crocker 24th July 1994*

A desperate climb up the groove and crack, snatching your way through the sequence.

## RIGHT-HAND SIDE

### 13 The Flight of Icarus — 18m F6c

*FA Adrian Berry & John Bullock 1990*

An excellent route. Head up the corner to the roof and make bold moves out right to gain the upper laybacks into the open groove above.

### 14 St Elmo's Fire — 14m F6a+

*FA Roy Thomas & Phil Davies August 2009*

Shares a start with *Cat Nap*. From the ledge climb the red wall, swinging left onto the face climbing with interest to the shared lower off with *The Flight of Icarus*.

### 15 Cat Nap — 15m F6a+

*FA Roy Thomas & Nick O'Neil July 2009*

Climb to the ledge, then the red wall above taking on the old school crack and chimney.

### 16 Power Nap — 15m F7b

*FA Simon Rawlinson March 2008*

Easy beginnings to a ledge lead to a short bouldery sequence on crimps and a gaston to reach the finale. Tough despite the half-height rest. Single bolt lower off.

### 17 Snooze Control — 12m F6a
*FA Roy Thomas & Richie Phillips 2009*

Have a clipstick handy for the first bolt. Begin off balance before better holds lead up the groove, ending with tricky layback finish to the lower off.

### 18 Sleep Easy — 15m F7b
*FA Adam Shore & Simon Rawlinson March 2007*

Good technical, sequencey climbing throughout with a distinct crux. Climb the centre of the slab to a ledge. Pause here before some technical moves lead you to the top of the arête. Turn the roof on its right side to finish.

The path now leads up steps to the following routes.

### 19 R.E.M. Sleep — 15m F6a
*FA Roy Thomas & Myles Jordan 2009*

A hanging thread at the top of the route identifies this line. Feisty moves through the bottom corner lead to an easier angle before steepening towards the distant and hard-to-reach belay.

### 20 White Slider — 10m F6a+
*FA Roy Thomas & Richie Phillips 2009*

Clipstick useful for the start. An awkward start onto the block leads to good wall climbing up the white streak. Bear right around the corner to a balancey finish to the shared lower off. (The name is a play on words from the famous Eiger North Face route).

### 21 Project — 10m
*FA Yet to Be*

Closed project; please do not climb.

### 22 Miami Vice — 18m F6c
*FA Adam Shore & Simon Rawlinson March 2007*

If done in summer months, the bay will be filled with boats. Start from the floor (not the ledge). Some powerful moves will take you to a little rest before some delicate slab moves working right and then left take you to the top.

### 23 Coronal Discharge — 16m F6a+
*FA Roy Thomas & Chris Wyatt 2009*

A relatively easy start for a change. Make moves up and through the groove on laybacks before trending right to the lower off.

### 24 Wakey Wakey — 16m F5+
*FA Roy Thomas & Chris Wyatt 2009*

A straightforward start leads you into the deceptive ledge system with good wall climbing. Take care with some wobbly rock.

### 25 Take it Easy — 15m F5+
*FA Adam Shore June 2007*

Takes the final line on the main section and the well-featured wall.

### FIN

This prominent arête all on its lonesome is considered by some to be the best route at the venue.

### 26 Fin — 10m F8a
*FA Adrian Berry 1994*

A seriously hard boulder start leads into a gritstone-esque balance affair. This doesn't suffer the seepage problem and is rarely dirty.

Jo Pollard at one of the intricacies
of the Sewerpipe area.
Photo: Stuart Llewellyn.

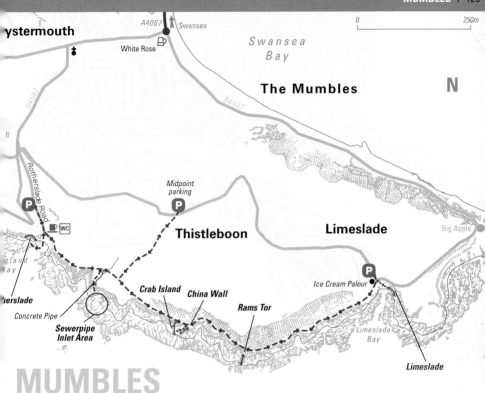

# MUMBLES

Some little gems lie round the corner from the Mumbles pier, located on the western tip of Swansea Bay. Their proximity to Swansea and rugged setting makes for a great combination. This jagged stretch of coastline has numerous opportunities for bouldering, as well as some sport and trad routes.

This area has the best bouldering Gower has to offer. Caswell has to be king of convenience climbing with easy access to the bay, beach huts and cafe, and oodles to climb. Rotherslade has some very good problems just around the corner from a great family beach, with a cafe at the top of the promenade steps. A little further on, the Sewerpipe Inlet area is worth seeking out with its hours of entertaining problems. China Wall is a useful non-tidal bouldering spot. Limeslade has very quick access for those who want a good short session. The Old Bridge offers easy access bouldering in the heart of the city, straight off the beach on quality sandstone blocks. Crab Island is a substantial piece of quality rock with a good

low- to mid-grade spread of traditional climbs. Rams Tor, another significant bit of rock, boasts high-level fully bolted sport routes. What's more, there's also an ice cream parlour at the start of the short approach!

**Approaches**: With the exception of Caswell, all areas described in this chapter are easily reached from the coastal path seen on the map above. The approaches are described assuming you've parked at the closest spot. It's worth noting that Rotherslade Road parking spaces fill up early in the summer period, and the alternative midpoint parking may be your best option.

**Caswell:** Head into Mumbles. At the mini-roundabout by the White Rose pub, turn right heading uphill through a long street of shops (B4593). At the traffic lights turn left passing a church. Continue on this road uphill for half a mile, passing the other climbing areas on the left (Rotherslade Road parking). Continue following signposts for 'Caswell Bay' for 1 mile to a pay-and-display car park.

**Rotherslade Road parking:** Approach as per Caswell. Where the road uphill widens with central reservations at the brow of the hill, turn left following signposts for Rotherslade. Continue down Rotherslade Road, and park here. Walking downhill brings you onto a promenade with a café; the coastal path is on the left.

**Alternative midpoint parking:** If there are no spaces at the site described above, go back up Rotherslade Road and take the right turn. Go uphill with another central reservation with trees in its middle. After half a mile, the road kinks right into a single lane but immediately widens. Park sensibly around here. A gate and coastal path signs can be seen next to house no.104. Go through fields following well-worn trails to take you to the coastal path, passing a house with a green-tiled roof.

**Limeslade parking:** Head into Mumbles and at the mini-roundabout go straight on. Follow the coast road around, passing the Big Apple. Continue on the road to its end at Limeslade Bay. Park on the road just right of Forte's ice-cream parlour. Just beyond the parlour and some flats is the start of the coastal path.

Sewerpipe Inlet

**Rotherslade:** From the cafe near the Rotherslade Road parking, take the large concrete steps onto the beach. The small bouldering cove is round to the right of the big rock in the middle of beach.

**Sewerpipe Inlet:** This can be difficult to find on your first visit, but keep an eye out for a long concrete pipe from the land out towards the sea. From the Rotherslade café, walk along the coastal path for 5 minutes until a path junction above a small cove is reached. Just beyond this follow a trail through vegetation to bring you to the top of a well-worn gully with the concrete pipe. Follow this pipe down and bear left into the inlet shown on the approach photo.

Mumbles lighthouse.

**Crab Island:** From the Rotherslade café, walk the coastal path passing a signposted junction (the alternative midpoint approach). At the start of a series of railings, peel of right down a well-eroded bank to the top of the crag.

**China Wall:** As for Crab Island, but continue on the coastal past a second set of railings. Where the coastal path bends to the left, follow a well-worn path down onto a rocky platform. Scramble right, back on yourself continuing around to the base of the wall. China Wall bouldering can also be accessed from the top of Crab Island crag by crossing the large jammed block bridge onto the rocky platform.

**Rams Tor:** From the ice-cream parlour, follow the coastal path for around 5 minutes until at the top of the steps; the crag appears on your left in the gully below. The base is gained either by scrambling down to the right on a steep path through dense sharp gorse (not for those in shorts), or less painfully to the left and abseil down the crag.

**Limeslade Bay:** From the Limeslade parking spot by the ice-cream parlour, head down the steps onto the beach. The bouldering is round to the left in its own small bay.

**The Old Bridge:** Set on Swansea Bay sea front in the middle of the bay, the old slip bridge is best accessed from the car parks or street parking around by the Guild Hall. This is found by turning off the sea-front road at the junction by the bridge.

The name Mumbles refers not to the Victorian seaside resort of Oystermouth, but to the two islands that lead out into Swansea Bay. The name itself comes from the Latin word *Mamilae* which in French is Mambles. This translates into English as Mammaries, a cheeky reference to the shape of the two perky headlands.

# CASWELL

Caswell Bay is one of Gower's most visited beaches for families, sun-worshippers and surfers. The bay will be very busy during the summer due to its easy parking, access, beach hut shops and cafe. With the tide out you'll be able to find a little corner to escape the onlooking stares. Alternatively, find an area in plain sight and satisfy your inner rock god. The areas close to the promenade steps are likely to be busy with people, so please avoid squashing small children and sand castles. The bouldering on offer ranges from pleasant traverse walls above golden sands to topping out of a lone boulder above horrendous landings; bring as many pads and spotters as can be accrued. The tide comes in right the way up to the beach steps, so tidal access to the different areas ranges massively.

**The Block** boasts well-featured arêtes and a back wall, and **Platform Wall** is a crimpy overhanging featured wall. **Quartz Wall** is a good place to start for warm-up traverses and wall problems. **Black Rift** is where to head for overhanging challenges. You will find an arête and crossly wall problems at **The Towers**. **Corner Bay** offers both wall and arête climbing above pebbles. **Thread Bay** provides good climbing through overlaps.

SS 5930 8763

**Aspect**: N, S, E and W

1. THE BLOCK

2. PLATFORM WALL

1. 2.

3. QUARTZ WALL

5. THE TOWERS

4. BLACK RIFT

8. CORNER BAY

7. THREAD BAY

3.     4.     5.     6.     7.

Concrete steps

# ROTHERSLADE

Rotherslade provides an ideal little spot for combining some bouldering and a day at the beach, with the convenience of having a café within eyesight. There's a decent mixture of problems in the cove and one or two are highball. Access can be obtained 3 hours either side of low tide.

SS 6100 8732

**Aspect**: E, S and W

# SEWERPIPE INLET

Sewerpipe Inlet has the largest selection of good bouldering on Gower, with many little intricacies. The water-worn rocks have a mixture of wave-smoothed sloping rock, rather sharp edges or positive jugs in between. The pebbly landings generally require mats and good spotters for some of the higher challenges. The height of these pebbles can change significantly, making things a little more challenging. The entire area is covered at high tide, with access possible about 2 hours 30 mins either side of low tide.

SS 6126 8709

**Aspect**: N, S, E and W

The classic problem of the area is *Fridge Hugger*, a sit start on an overhung slopey arête which is well worth seeking out.

Charles Romijn

© Donna Carless bouldering at China Wall.
Photo: Stuart Llewellyn.

# CHINA WALL

China Wall is a useful non-tidal venue which is big enough to keep you entertained for a couple of hours. This short wall sweeps up from a rocky platform and is vertical on its right-hand side. Its angle and difficulties increase as it sweeps left into a small overhanging section. A word of warning: take care if you choose to top out, as the rock is rather fracturous at the top. The holds are generally kinder than the barnacle-covered tidal bouldering spots.

SS 6163 8695

**Aspect**: NW

© Limeslade boulde
Photo: Mike Britto

# THE OLD BRIDGE

Set on Swansea Bay seafront near the heart of the city, the old Victorian bridge supports provide some entertaining bouldering off the beach. A mix of challenging traverses and highball problems on sandstone blocks give a pleasant local training spot that combines well with a BBQ and friends.

SS 6432 9217

**Aspect**: S

# LIMESLADE

Limeslade is a convenient venue with a handful of highball walls and some steep smooth challenges. The rock dries fast, although the central walls can seep after rain. The pebbly landings are much more pleasant with a mat. Access can be obtained 3 hours either side of low tide.

SS 6255 8711

**Aspect**: S

 Crab Island gap

# CRAB ISLAND

Crab Island is not to be overlooked as it has some great climbing on good rock. It's proximity to Swansea only adds to its appeal, allowing you to bag a few routes when time is tight. The venue is tidal, and is accessible 2 hours 30 mins either side of low water. An abseil can be made from stakes above the back wall into the landward corner of the crag, allowing you access to the walls before the tide is out far enough to walk in along the base of the crag. If visiting during the summer months, note that the face is used by the local kids as a cliff-jumping spot (hence the array of abandoned socks). This was known as Rams Tor Crag in previous guidebooks. The top of the crag is not particularly forthcoming when searching for a bomber belay, but if you keep searching you will find something of use. There are also a few old pegs available, which should always be backed up.

SS 6159 8694

**Aspect**: W

**1 Suicide Groove**      **21m HVS 5b**

*FA H. Jones, D. Bowman & A. Wilson 1985*

Start at the back of the zawn just left of the cave. Layback the often wet groove and traverse delicately right on the smooth ramp to gain the main corner. Continue up this past brilliant flowstone features to the roof. A puzzling traverse out right leads to the top.

> The next few routes are started by overcoming the gap between the large boulder and the wall as the base of the crag is undercut and washed smooth. If needed, the step can be protected with a lassoed sling around a spike.

**2 Fat Crack**      **19m VS 4b**

*FA H. Jones, D. Bowman & A. Wilson 1985*

Climb the massive wide crack on the left of the main face, with surprisingly small gear.

*Something's on the Wall* (VS 4c),
and it's one of the authors.
Photo: Stuart Llewellyn.

### ③ Something's on the Wall      18m VS 4c

*FA H. Jones, D. Bowman & A. Wilson 1985*

Traverse left from the boulder step and climb the wall to the right of *Fat Crack*. Take care with fragile rock at the top.

### ④ Romey      15m HS 4a

*FA H. Jones, D. Bowman & A. Wilson 1985*

Make moves left from the step over until underneath a short vertical crack, then climb a direct line to the top.

### ⑤ Something's on the Move      15m S

*FA H. Jones, D. Bowman & A. Wilson 1985*

After launching from the boulder, climb straight up to a small niche on good holds then direct to the top with good gear after the step onto the face.

### ⑥ Lizzetta's Route      14m HS 4a

*FA H. Jones, D. Bowman & A. Wilson 1985*

Move to the right from the boulder step and climb up the wall direct.

### ⑦ Stormwatch      15m HS 4b

*FA H. Jones, D. Bowman & A. Wilson 1985*

A grand route with a bouldery start on massive holds leads into a small cave. Next take the faint cracks above where the angle eases off.

### ⑧ Unknown      11m S

*FA Unknown*

Climb the arête on the right of the main wall, after a scramble start to the ledge.

### ⑨ Space Oddity      19m HVS 4c

*FA H. Jones, D. Bowman & A. Wilson 1985*

Gain the ledge to start, then pull boldly round onto the cliff face to begin your rising adventure. Finish on the left side of the crag just past *Fat Crack*, with a bold finale.

### ⑩ Where Did You Get That Girly Voice? 10m VS 4c

*FA Martyn Richards 1994*

Take the steepening arête left of *Oyster Bubble*'s corner, with some fiddly gear.

### ⑪ Oyster Bubble      10m VS 4b

*FA H. Jones, D. Bowman & A. Wilson 1985*

Climb the rightwards-facing corner.

### ⑫ Muttley      9m VS 5a

*FA H. Jones, D. Bowman & A. Wilson 1985*

Take the crack which runs through and to the top of the wall.

### ⑬ Dastardly      9m E1 5b

*FA H. Jones, D. Bowman & A. Wilson 1985*

Climb the crack in the bulge, avoiding features of *Muttley*.

# RAMS TOR

This sweep of west-facing limestone is a tale of two halves from its prominent feature, a large roof below a subtle-angled slab. Many of the climbs' challenges are the transition between these two contrasting styles as the climber attempts to get established on the upper slab, although the initial wall is no pushover.

The venue is pretty much non-tidal except for routes right of *Nostradamus*, which are typically available 2 hours 30 mins either side of lower water. That said, if the seas are particularly rough you may get a soaking anyway. It receives afternoon and evening sun, and is generally sheltered from the wind. A clip stick is useful at this venue.

Belay stakes are available above the crag for those wanting to avoid the steep gorse approach. The first three routes have seen a lot of cleaning and the removal of loose rock but some may still be encountered; please take care.

SS 6189 8680
**Aspect**: W

### 1 Rampage                              16m F7a+

*FA Bill Gregory 17th October 2009*

A mega-steep route, but luckily with mostly jugs to pull on. Ends with a hard move at the top to pockets.

### 2 The Constant Gardener                18m F6c+

*FA Bill Gregory 13th July 2009*

Another steep outing with good holds. Starts at a conglomerate ledge.

### 3 Air Display                          18m F7a+

*FA Alan Rosier 25th July 2009*

Climb up and to a large flake and into the cleaned corner. A sturdy technical finish awaits.

### 4 The Cool Crux Clan                   15m F7a

*FA Adrian Berry & Geraint Morris 1993*

Gower's first intended clip-up sport route, originally drilled by hand. A more vertical affair, but with a few surprises in store.

### 5 Ride the Funky Wave, Babe            16m F7a

*FA Adrian Berry & Nigel Thomas 1992*

A popular climb that starts at the left edge of the cliff's distinct roof. Boulder through the roof, then pull up onto and dance the slab to the lower off

### 6 Rain Dance 16m F7b
*FA Adrian Berry & Paul Christie 1993*

The roof is gained with a juggy start before a hard fingery pull onto the slab.

### 7 Hypocritical Mass 14m F7b+
*FA Adrian Berry 1993*

A stiff start to the roof leads into a second difficult section, turning the lip of the overhang.

### 8 Renaissance 14m F6c+
*FA Adrian Berry 21st December 2008*

Marred by the need to clip-stick the first bolt and pull on the rope to a jug to start. Good holds take the climber to a large jug on the lip; a difficult pull unlocks the slab above.

### 9 Captain Hook 15m F7b
*FA Adrian Berry 1993*

A link-up starting as for *Nostradamus* and finishing up *Renaissance*.

### 10 Nostradamus 17m F7b
*FA Adrian Berry 1993*

An excellent route. Start with demanding moves through the overhanging bands. A rest on a big ledge can be had before taking on the roof. The main challenge is turning the lip.

### 11 The Loneliness of the Long Distance Runner 14m F7b
*FA Adrian Berry & Nigel Thomas 1993*

A massively positive ape index is needed for the reach around the roof, with some thuggy moves.

### 12 Totally Clips 15m F7c
*FA Adrian Berry 1993*

The hardest route here, with powerful and technical moves.

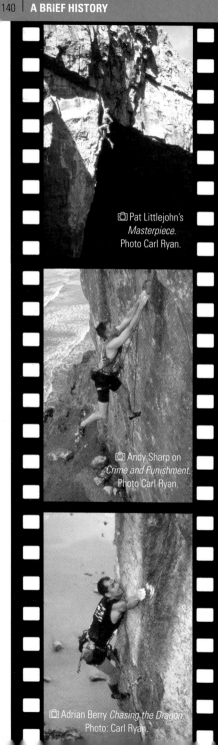

📷 Pat Littlejohn's *Masterpiece*. Photo Carl Ryan.

📷 Andy Sharp on *Crime and Punishment*. Photo Carl Ryan.

📷 Adrian Berry *Chasing the Dragon*. Photo: Carl Ryan.

# A BRIEF HISTORY

Records of people climbing on Gower go back to the late 1940s when routes such as *Classic* (HD) and *Dulfer* (S 4a) on Boiler Slab were established. Development was slow and it was not until the mid-1950s and the arrival of John Brailsford that routes started to come thick and fast. Along with the St Athan Mountain Rescue Team, he explored the Three Cliffs and Tor Bay and gave Gower its first VS with the classic *Scavenger* (VS 4c).

The late 1950s brought Jeremy Talbot to the scene, who probably has as many new routes to his name as everyone else put together. With a variety of partners he climbed the lower sea cliffs of Gower extensively, and later produced the first guide book to the area which was published in 1970.

The 1960s saw change, with members of Swansea University's Mountaineering Club including Eryl Pardoe looking to the higher cliffs of Fall Bay and Pennard, adding the area's first E3 with *V Groove* (E3 5c).

"New climbs are constantly being found, but it would seem that the area has now been so extensively covered there is relatively little of merit left to be done," wrote Jeremy Talbot in his 1970 Gower guide before Paviland, Juniper Wall, Oxwich or Foxhole had seen any ascents.

The peninsula's standard of climbing took a huge step forward with the arrival of Pat Littlejohn in the early 1970s, who freed hard routes previously climbed with aid such as *Yellow Wall* (E3 5c) and *Transformer* (E3 6a) on Yellow Wall, Fall Bay.

While Talbot was busy developing Paviland in the 1970s, the South Wales Mountaineering Club and other local climbers John Bullock and Roy Thomas started to make their mark on the area with classic lines such as *Assassin* (HVS 5a) at Juniper Wall. The team of Gwyn Evans and John Bullock would leave many fantastic climbs at this crag and at Pennard within the HVS–E4 bracket.

The 1980s saw another guide released, and hundreds of new routes being put up in the area. Standards were raised once more with Andy Sharp and John Harwood continuing to push the boundaries by freeing old aid routes to create hard test pieces in places such as Trial Wall at Rhossili. Pat Littlejohn took time away from the flurry of development at the up-and-coming Pembroke to give Gower its first E6 with *Masterpiece* (E6 6b). During this period Martin Crocker brought the serious *The Thurba Pillar* (E5 6b) to the adventurous Thurba Head in addition to several impressive lines at Gower's showpiece crag, Yellow Wall.

The 1990s saw a changing ethic come to the area. After a local bolt debate in 1994, a series of fully bolted sports routes were established. Roy Thomas and Martin Crocker saw the potential at Pwlldu, where Martin developed *Senser* giving the first Gower F8a (although quickly accepted as F7c+). The pace of development at other suitable sites was hindered however; although the climbing fraternity had a bolting agreement, access issues emerged with the landowners being unhappy about developments.

With the situation resolved a few years later, Oxwich's potential was unleashed mainly by the unrelenting efforts of Roy Thomas and Gary Gibson. Foxhole's development ensued, with Goi Ashmore climbing the brilliant *Pioneers of the Hypnotic Groove* (F7b) and succeeding with his project *Palace of Swords Reversed* (F8a). Prior to the millennium, Martin Crocker returned to Thurba Head to enhance his legacy with *Unearthly Power* (E5 6c). However the route that increased the E numbers threshold on Gower would be Adrian Berry's *Chasing the Dragon* (E8 6c) on Yellow Wall.

The new century saw another new guide in 2003 and new routes are still coming thick and fast. In the last few years John Bullock and Danny McCarrol saw Southgate's potential for entry-level sport climbing, and retro-bolted some less-frequented venues. This was followed with the new sports crag of Bowen's Parlour and the reopening of Minchin Hole after a 10 year ban. Oxwich suffered a major rockfall, destroying some of the area's hardest sport climbs. These were however replaced with one of the last independent lines at Foxhole in Simon Rawlinson's unrepeated *Surplomb de Ray* (F8b). Adrian Berry and Simon later joined forces to develop Zulu Zawn, giving *Zulu Wall* (F8a) and *Ultimatum* (F7c). At the end of

Gary Gibson's *Man of Earth*.
Photo Carl Ryan.

Simon Rawlinson on *Surplomb de Ray*.
Photo: Make The Next Move Images.

this decade Adrian released a Rockfax mini-guide to the area, a well-needed update.

This is of course just a whistle-stop tour of the past 60 years of Gower climbing history; far more climbing has taken place than we could ever document in such a short space. Indeed, even as we finish writing this guide, it is already becoming outdated by new routes of all styles thanks to the efforts of dedicated climbers continuing our bond with the peninsula. We hope the crags we've hand-picked for this select guide provide you with your own memories of this stunning stretch of the South Wales coastline. See you at the crags!

# Route Index